READING
CONNECTIONS

SKILLS AND STRATEGIES FOR PURPOSEFUL READING

INTERMEDIATE

ANNE EDIGER and CHERYL PAVLIK

OXFORD

Oxford University Press
198 Madison Avenue
New York, NY 10016 USA

Great Clarendon Street
Oxford OX2 6DP England

Oxford New York

*Athens Auckland Bangkok Bogota Buenos Aires
Calcutta Cape Town Chennai Dar es Salaam
Delhi Florence Hong Kong Istanbul Karachi
Kuala Lumpur Madrid Melbourne Mexico City
Mumbai Nairobi Paris São Paulo Shanghai
Singapore Taipei Tokyo Toronto Warsaw*

and associated companies in
Berlin Ibadan

OXFORD is a trademark of Oxford University Press.

ISBN 0-19-435825-9

Library of Congress Cataloging-in-Publication Data
Ediger, Anne.
   Reading connections. Intermediate book / Anne Ediger and
     Cheryl Pavlik. p. cm.
   Includes bibliographical references (p.).
   ISBN 0-19-435825-9 (student book) — ISBN 0-19-436732-0
   (answer key) 1. English language—Textbooks for foreign
   speakers. 2. Readers. I. Title. II. Pavlik, Cheryl, 1949–

   PE1128 . E348 1999
   428.6'4 21—dc21   99-043725

Editorial Manager: Susan Lanzano
Senior Acquisitions Editor: Janet Aitchison
Editor: Robin N. Longshaw
Production Editor: Klaus Jekeli
Editorial Assistants: Katharine Chandler and Justin Hartung
Design Project Manager: Lynne Torrey
Designer: Elizabeth Onorato
Interior Book Design: Shelley Himmelstein, Inc.
Art Buyer and Picture Researcher: Stacey Godlesky
Production Manager: Abram Hall
Production Coordinator: Shanta Persaud

Printing (last digit): 10 9 8 7 6 5 4 3

Printed in Hong Kong.

Acknowledgments

Illustrations and realia by Annie Bissett, Eliot Bergman,
Uldis Klavins, Elizabeth Onorato, Nina Wallace

Cover design by Mark C. Kellogg

Cover photo: Brian Pieters/Masterfile

*The publishers would like to thank the following for their
permission to reproduce photographs:* Sandy Hill/AP/Wide World
Photos; Jonathan Blair, Bob Krist, Richard T. Nowitz, Neal
Preston, Michael S. Yamashita/Corbis; Roger Viollet/Liaison
International; Jerry Bauer/Simon & Schuster; Superstock; 20th
Century Fox, MGM, Paramount/The Kobal Collection; Peter
Beck, Ed Bock, George Disario, Peter Fisher, Ronnie Kaufman,
Rob Lewine, Tom & Dee Ann McCarthy, Nancy Ney, Jose Pelaez,
Chuck Savage, Mug Shots, Ariel Skelley, Tom Stewart/The Stock
Market; Christopher Bissel, Peter Correz, Elie Bernager, Nicole
Katano, Jon Riley/Tony Stone Images

ACKNOWLEDGMENTS

We would like to thank all those at Oxford University Press who made this book possible, especially Janet Aitchison, Acquisitions Editor, and Robin Longshaw, our editor. We are also indebted to Justin Hartung and Katharine Chandler for their help with the often arduous permissions process.

Our heartfelt thanks also go out to Julie Landau and Susan Lanzano, who provided invaluable help and support during the conceptualization of the project.

We would also like to acknowledge our reviewers for their valuable comments and suggestions in developing this series. In particular, we wish to thank:

Roberta Alexander (San Diego City College)

Patricia Brenner

Linda Britton

Andy Cavanaugh (Maryland English Institute)

Gaye Childress (University of North Texas)

Byung-Eun Cho (Sung Kong Hoe University, Seoul, Korea)

Dr. Chung-tien Chou (National Taiwan Normal University, Taipei City, Taiwan)

Teresa Bruner Cox (Soai University, Osaka)

Kathy Flynn (Glendale Community College, California)

Cathy Garcia-Hill (Suffolk Community College, New York)

Jeffrey Grill

Lori Harrilla

Margaret Haynes (Delta College, Iowa)

Patty Heiser (University of Washington)

Cindy Hewitt (University of Tampa)

Carolyn Heacock (University of Kansas)

Pamela Kennedy (Holyoke Community College, Massachusetts)

Chuong Bae Kim (Korea University)

Julia Klein (Tunghai University, Taichung, Taiwan)

Javier E. Macuaga (Athenée Français, Tokyo)

Jean Martone (University of Washington)

Blanca Moss (El Paso Community College)

Denise Mussman (University of Missouri at St. Louis)

Elizabeth Neblett (Union County College, New Jersey)

Eugene Parulis (Community College of Vermont/World Learning, Inc.)

Peg Sarosy (San Francisco State University)

Kathy Sherak (San Francisco State University)

Barbara Smith-Palinkas

Stephanie Snider (Suffolk Community College, New York)

Amy Stotts-Ali (Tunghai University, Taichung, Taiwan)

Christine Tierney (Houston Community College, Texas)

Julie Un (Massasoit Community College, Massachusetts)

This book is dedicated to the memory of my father, Ferdinand Ediger, the first EFL teacher I ever knew. He was my first model as a teacher and my greatest model for life.

—AE

I would like to dedicate this book to my students of the past 25 years, who have taught me more about language learning than any book I've ever read, or any course that I have ever taken.

—CP

CONTENTS

READING STRATEGIES	STRATEGIES FOR UNKNOWN VOCABULARY	UNIT TASKS
Understanding how information is organized Finding the topic of each paragraph Dealing with technical readings Identifying the author's purpose Making inferences Looking for language signals Reading spoken language	Recognizing titles and names Looking for explanations of unknown words Understanding familiar words with special meanings Using affixes to guess meaning	Deciding who should care for the children

Examining organization: process
Understanding and using subtitles
Understanding organization
Understanding the format of a text
Understanding what words refer to:
    personal pronouns
    this and *that*
Summarizing
Examining organization
Understanding the author's tone
Understanding the use of examples
Looking for guiding sentences
	Using synonyms to guess words in context
	Using examples to guess words in context
	Understanding the general meaning of unknown words
		1. Film analysis
		2. Reviewing a movie

Using charts, graphs, and tables Understanding reference words Recognizing the important ideas of a text Understanding different levels of information	Deciding to use the dictionary Understanding dictionary entries Choosing the correct meaning Using general knowledge to guess the meaning of unknown words Understanding suffixes Recognizing related words and parts of speech	1. Giving financial advice 2. Evaluating your lifestyle
Learning how to read a textbook Understanding how examples support important ideas Recognizing important ideas	Using a dictionary and a glossary Choosing the best dictionary definition Understanding complex noun phrases Using a vocabulary decision tree	1. Figuring out your intelligence type and learning style 2. Evaluating your school experience

INTRODUCTION

TO THE TEACHER

SERIES OVERVIEW

Reading Connections is a two-volume Intermediate to High-Intermediate ESL reading series which teaches students active reading skills. It is for people studying to enter a college or university in an English-speaking country, for those studying to further their careers, as well as for those who simply want to be able to communicate more effectively.

Each of the two books in the series contains a Preview unit, which introduces students to basic concepts in reading more effectively, and four main units, each of which focuses on a different high-interest theme. Within each unit, an authentic purpose for reading is first set up, and then a variety of readings and exercises provides information and develops skills which will help the students accomplish their task. In each unit, students integrate and synthesize the information from the readings and apply it to their task.

Although the series is intended primarily for ESL reading courses, it may be used in courses where writing is taught as well. Many of the unit tasks may be performed either as oral or as written activities, and the series may be viewed as the core component in a reading-to-write approach to the teaching of academic literacy skills. Additional suggestions for each of these options is provided below under Classroom Strategies.

READING FOR A PURPOSE: A RATIONALE

When people read in the real world (in academic, business, or other contexts), a large part of the time they do not read simply for the sake of reading (although they may do this when they read for pleasure). Most of the time they are required to use their reading skills in order to accomplish some purpose. For example, people read in different ways when they want to

- find out a departure time and cost of a train or bus by scanning a timetable or brochure
- prepare to take a test or write a research paper in a college or university class by reading large amounts of material and synthesizing it
- set up a new computer or other piece of electronic equipment by reading carefully and following written instructions
- write (or present orally) a business proposal for a course of action in some area of their job by reading, analyzing, and synthesizing company reports and documents

In these kinds of reading, readers typically start out with an issue, a topic, an argument, or a hypothesis which is tied to their purpose, be it making a presentation, making a decision, confirming or rejecting a hypothesis, presenting research findings, or analyzing and then producing a better product. In order to find the necessary information, readers generally search through a variety of material (or it is presented to them by a supervisor in the form of company documents, or by an instructor in the form of lectures and textbook readings).

Usually, in the process of searching for this information, readers collect a number of texts, and skim them quickly, looking for anything related to the issue in each one. Sometimes readers find that a text is broadly related, but irrelevant to the specific need at hand. Sometimes the material is only partly relevant, and sometimes it is exactly on the topic. However, until they skim the material, readers may not know how useful it is. Occasionally, readers must go back and forth, searching for something that is relevant. Sometimes the material they find is very difficult to understand, and they must decide if it is worth wading through the tough, unfamiliar content, possibly even skipping sections, in the quest for the small bits of truly useful information. Generally, the result is that far more material is read than is actually useful for the task. Thus, readers must constantly ask themselves if the information is relevant or helpful to their purpose.

In purposeful reading, a reader needs to use a variety of strategies and skills. These include skimming material, scanning for useful information and making inferences about information. As a result, not all of the information available is read or utilized equally. Readers must constantly monitor their comprehension of what they have read, and evaluate how they need to read it, as well as which strategy to use when reading.

Thus, rather than focusing on reading for the purpose of learning grammar, vocabulary, and idioms in English, or even for practicing different reading skills, this book approaches reading as it is done in the real world. It provides learners with a specific purpose and a collection of readings which will help them accomplish it. This purpose then guides them toward reading for true meaning and understanding. Along the way, readers are given many opportunities to develop reading subskills as a support for arriving at meaning. They will be able to follow signaling words, make inferences, deal with words they don't understand, alternate between skimming, scanning, and other techniques, or appropriately use prediction.

In this series, students are also taught to be critical, active, and independent readers. This means helping students become more aware of what happens when they read, including understanding that reading is not a passive process: information does not merely flow in one direction from the page to the reader's brain. Students are taught to interact with text and to bring their own questions, ideas, and analyses to their reading, as well as to learn strategies for understanding more and reading faster.

In addition, after skills and strategies are taught, the amount of assistance is gently decreased through the book, encouraging students to try to use the skills on their own. This teaches the students to gradually perform the skills without assistance, so that they will be able to continue applying these skills even after their reading course is finished.

In many cases, students will find this approach quite new. It is important to explain why this approach is being taken, and to assure them that this way of reading works.

HOW THE SERIES IS ORGANIZED

To simulate the sort of reading required in content-area courses and real-life environments, this book is organized into four large themes (one in each unit), with six to eight related readings on each topic. Each collection of readings approximates what students might find in a textbook on a single subject area—a collection of articles or a group of other documents related to a task. There are a number of reasons for including a large number of readings:

- They resemble authentic reading tasks encountered by students in content-based courses at the college/university level and in business.
- The numerous articles/readings on a single topic help students gradually develop topic-related and subtechnical vocabulary and other related language skills necessary for handling the oral and written discussion of an issue.
- They provide a substantial body of informational content which must be understood, weighed and synthesized, just as real tasks require. In addition, it enables different students to select somewhat different material on which to focus. Students must also utilize their critical thinking skills to justify their choices.
- They bring together reading material from a variety of genres, in order to help students become familiar with the different writing styles and patterns, typical language usage,

methods of organization, formats, and presentation of information that characterizes each of these genres. Because the readings come from a variety of genres, they will not all have the same format or even difficulty level (though they have been roughly tuned to the same level); students need to learn and use strategies to deal with the specific problems that each presents along the way.

CLASSROOM STRATEGIES

Unit Format

The units in this book have the following general format:

Unit One
  Part A: Reading for a Purpose
    Identify the Information You Need
    Readings 1 to 7
  Part B: Doing the Unit Task
    Thinking About Reading for a Purpose
  Part C: Expansion Activities
    Applying Your Knowledge
    The Electronic Link
    For More Information
    Essay Questions
    Evaluating Your Progress
    Setting Your Reading Goals

Units Two to Four
  Part A: Unit Task 1
    Identify the Information You Need
    Readings 1 to 3
    Unit Task 1
  Part B: Unit Task 2
    Identify the Information You Need
    Readings 4 to 6
    Unit Task 2
  Part C: Expansion Activities
    Applying Your Knowledge
    The Electronic Link
    For More Information
    Essay Questions
    Evaluating Your Progress
    Setting Your Reading Goals

Unit Features

The Unit Task Each unit in the book covers a different theme and thus may stand alone. However, it is recommended that the units be covered in the order presented. This is because individual skills are taught in detail at the point where they are first introduced, and then they reappear with minimal explanation for additional practice (or as margin questions) in later readings.

Each unit begins by establishing a purpose for reading. Unit One introduces this concept, and students will use it to decide how they will read and to determine the usefulness (or irrelevance) of what they are reading. After each reading, students are guided toward finding the key information that they will need to identify in a particular passage so that they can accomplish their purpose.

The students' attention is focused on the purpose for reading in three specific ways: 1) the presentation of the Unit Task, 2) the exercises before and after each reading that check understanding of key concepts and focus on these crucial points, and 3) activities/exercises that require the reader to determine which information in each reading (if any) is relevant and then ask the student to do something with the relevant information (e.g., synthesize, conclude, decide, analyze, or apply).

With several of the strategies and skills (e.g., Previewing, Understanding How Information is Organized), the student is given a great deal of assistance in earlier units, but later, explicit instruction for these strategies is decreased. Since the material is geared toward building knowledge, reading, and language skills over the course of a unit and over the course of the book, teaching the units in sequence will ensure that students receive the maximum benefit from their use. In addition, it may be helpful to know the location where each strategy is first introduced (see the Table of Contents).

Skill Development With each passage, the students' attention is focused on comprehending so that they can accomplish their purpose. Specific reading skills and strategies are taught in the context of particular readings as they are needed for comprehending that reading. These strategies help learners to develop the sub-skills which underlie and facilitate the accomplishment of the larger goal, including various strategies for handling unknown vocabulary, skimming and scanning, predicting, making inferences, understanding organization, identifying cohesive ties and transition words, and activating background knowledge. Since the accomplishment of the larger purpose or task is of primary importance, the development of the sub-skills should be viewed as the *means* which facilitate this, not as the *end goal* of students' learning to read in English. In each exercise, the skill development is oriented toward understanding the broader content.

Exercises Accompanying Each Reading Each of the readings in every unit has approximately the same format, as shown below. Because the choice of which specific strategy or skill should be focused on grew out of the specific content of each reading, there are a few readings which do not contain all of the exercises.

Step 1: Preview the Reading (and Previewing Strategies, with some readings)
Step 2: Read Closely
The Reading
Checking Your Comprehension
Making Inferences (not with every reading)
Topics for Discussion
Reading Strategies
Strategies for Unknown Vocabulary (not with every reading)
Step 3: Note Useful Information
Building Your Vocabulary
Writing Your Ideas (not with every reading)
Making Connections (not with every reading)

The Treatment of Unknown Vocabulary The handling of unknown vocabulary is one of the most troublesome aspects of reading in a second or foreign language. Typically, nonfluent readers want to look up every unknown word; otherwise, they often feel they are unable to understand any of what they are reading. Unfortunately, this constant use of a dictionary detracts from the meaningful comprehension of what is read, and forces the student into a word-by-word reading style quite contrary to the type of academic reading they will need in the future. Thus, the development of strategies for reading and synthesizing large amounts of text has been given prominent focus in this series.

There is also now much evidence from reading research that the development of new vocabulary is greatly facilitated through extensive (as opposed to intensive) reading and through extended contact with the written language. Thus, while the development of specific vocabulary is given a relatively small role in this book, a great deal of attention is paid to more broadly applicable vocabulary development skills. These include looking for patterns among related words, analyzing word parts, and identifying related word forms and word families. At the same time, students and teachers are encouraged to use any and all techniques available to them to learn new vocabulary, and students are encouraged to share with their classmates their own strategies. Since different students tend to need to learn different vocabulary, each student is encouraged to develop his or her own list of new vocabulary. Each unit includes suggestions for identifying, practicing, and remembering these new words.

Suggestions for Teaching

The Unit Task In Unit 1, the notion of reading for a purpose is introduced, and students are asked to read all seven readings, so that they find and synthesize the information they will need in order to accomplish the single Unit Task. Because this central notion of having a purpose for reading may be quite new for many students (and even teachers), teachers are encouraged to go through Unit One first, paying special attention to introducing the concept of a Unit Task and focusing students' attention on it frequently. Because many of the readings in this unit are quite short, and because of the nature of the Unit Task, students should be able to bring together the information from all of the readings. In Units 2–4, however, the readings become somewhat longer, and thus, the units are divided roughly in half, with a separate (but related) Unit Task for each group of three readings. The information used for the first Unit Task may also be useful for the second Unit Task. Each Unit Task should be focused on carefully by the class before reading, in order to set up the guiding purpose for which students will need to look for information as they go along. It is important that teachers bring the class's attention back to this task or purpose repeatedly and help students learn how to identify the information that will be useful for accomplishing their purpose.

There are several options for performing each Unit Task. The class may debate an issue (in a formal or informal oral debate), be asked to reach a consensus through discussion, make oral presentations, or write a paper presenting their analysis and synthesis. Also, students may be asked to do the task individually, in pairs, or in small groups.

Identify the Information You Need After being given the Unit Task, students are asked to predict the kinds of information they will need to find in order to accomplish the task and where they think they will find it. Instead of thinking in terms of "right" or "wrong," teachers are encouraged to guide students toward "reasonable" and away from "unreasonable" predictions. Then, after com-

pleting the readings, students should go back and review the predictions they originally made, to see if they have any new insights about which information will be useful for the task. This is a good time to discuss where and why their predictions may have been made. The ultimate goal of these exercises is to teach students to create and revise their own predictions.

Previewing (pre-reading) Exercises Before reading a text, students are asked to answer a series of questions designed to prepare them for the reading and improve their understanding. Some of the important skills include
- identifying the general topic of a reading
- determining what general knowledge they already have on this topic
- learning what the format of a text can tell them about how information will be presented or organized in the text
- understanding how a particular genre or source of a reading can influence their understanding or interpretation

However, instead of simply providing previewing questions for the students, this text teaches students how to preview texts by themselves. The teacher's goal should be to teach students the skills of pre-reading and predicting so that they will be able to do this on their own after their reading course is finished. After teaching students to preview at the beginning of the book, as they progress through the units they are gently encouraged to do it increasingly on their own, and by the last unit students are only given brief reminders about what they need to do before reading.

Margin Questions The margin questions accompanying most of the readings are not intended to be used the first time a passage is read. Instead, students should first try to read a passage on their own at least once, and then go through the passage again, making use of the questions in the margins.

The margin questions are thus designed to serve several purposes. First, they focus the students' attention on key content issues that each particular reading presents. Second, they recycle skills and strategies learned previously. Third, they model for students how they should be reading and provide clues and hints on how to do this. Students should thus be urged to read each passage several times (as needed).

Checking Your Comprehension This section is intended to be in most cases a general comprehension check, focusing on the key ideas in a reading. Detailed comprehension of the parts of the reading which contribute useful information toward accomplishing the Unit Task will actually come later, when students synthesize what they have read.

Topics for Discussion These are optional questions which push the students to express their own ideas on issues raised in the readings. They are not intended to be comprehension questions but "thinking questions" that grow naturally out of a reading and require students to make use of vocabulary and information presented in the reading while engaging them in critical thinking about what they have read. These questions may also be used as topics for written journal entries or compositions (either after or instead of oral discussion).

Reading Strategies After most of the readings, several reading strategy teaching points and related practice exercises are provided. These exercises teach students key skills and strategies for making sense of what they read and finding the information they need for the Unit Tasks. These strategies range from identifying important ideas, learning how examples support generalizations, and understanding how texts are organized, to learning to make inferences. When they focus students' attention on main ideas, these exercises avoid a common misconception that all readings have a single main idea. Rather, students are taught that in any passage, different kinds of information are of relative importance and that they need to identify the difference. Students are also taught that the information that an author may consider to be important may not be the information that they will find most useful for their purpose. Thus, these two different ways of identifying "important" information need to be distinguished and understood separately.

Strategies for Unknown Vocabulary After most readings, there are several exercises that help students deal with unknown words they encounter. These exercises encourage students to develop strategies that they can use as they are reading. They are intended to help students obtain meaning from what they read. In each case, they focus the students' attention on strategies that will be useful for that particular reading. Teachers should encourage students to think about and share with the class any other strategies they find useful for dealing with unknown words.

Building Your Vocabulary In this section, students are encouraged to build their own lists of vocabulary items that they want or need to learn (their personal vocabulary list), using the readings as a source of new words. Since the students' lists will vary somewhat, the teacher should check up on each student to see if he or she is indeed keeping an up-to-date list and learning it. For this purpose, teachers may wish to develop different exercises or methods of assessment, including the following:

- Based upon a list that each student provides to the teacher, the teacher (or other students) makes up a number of sentences to be used as a quiz on those words.
- The class may (as a group) write sentences using words from all of their lists and put the sentences into a "sentence bank" from which quizzes are later made up.

- Groups of students may be asked to use their words in summaries of specific readings (or to answer some of the questions in the Writing Your Ideas section of each unit).
- The teacher may from time to time ask individual students to share with the class what strategies they use to remember specific new words. These may include various mnemonic devices, individual strategies (e.g., "the word sounds like ___ in my native language"), or other learning techniques a student may have used.

Writing Your Ideas These topics are provided as additional, optional activities that ask students to put their ideas into written form. These are good places for students to practice using some of their new vocabulary from their personal vocabulary lists. While these are presented in the form of written activities, they may also be used for oral discussions or as informal journal entry topics. Some of them also lend themselves to paired writing activities, in which two students first discuss their responses orally and then write their ideas down collaboratively.

Making Connections These activities ask students to bring together or compare the ideas from several of the readings they have done. In some cases, they even require students to go back to previous units to make these comparisons. These are also places for students to recycle vocabulary.

Expansion Activities, Applying Your Knowledge, The Electronic Link, and Essay Questions These activities may be assigned as homework, with the students' findings later presented back to the class, or they may be assigned as a follow-up activity to be performed by the whole class. They provide additional oral, written, and extensive reading activities to supplement those in the unit. The Electronic Link activities may also be used to supplement the information from the unit. Looking for and reading information on the Internet is an excellent way to motivate students and to provide them with extensive reading opportunities (particularly in programs or countries where additional printed reading materials are difficult to obtain). An interesting takeoff on this idea would be to establish an e-mail exchange with another class that uses *Reading Connections* as their text and to have students share their final Unit Task reports or findings.

Evaluating Your Progress These self-check activities focus students' attention on the specific skills that were presented in each unit and ask students to rate their progress. This fits in with the overall aim of this book to teach students to take note of their own reading strategies and to become more aware of how (and how well) they are reading. By collecting information on the areas that students are still having trouble with, teachers can determine which areas the class needs more practice in and devise ways to provide practice.

Additional Readings An appendix of additional readings has been provided to accompany each unit. These readings may be used in a variety of ways, including as additional resources for

- assessing students' grasp of reading strategies, strategies for unknown vocabulary, or other skills learned in that unit by having students apply them to a related, but "new" text,
- providing even more information for the Unit Task,
- offering additional extensive reading on the same topic,
- complementing teachers' own exercises for more practice on specific strategies or skills.

Class Work versus Homework

Because many of the activities in this text ask students to try to read in ways which may be new to them, teachers are advised to model in class how such activities should be performed. Although some teachers feel that class time should not be spent on reading silently, it is precisely here that teachers can benefit from observing first-hand how their students are reading. Students will also benefit greatly from having their instructors model for them through a think-aloud procedure what is going on in the teacher's mind as he or she reads new material in English.

Certain activities should be done in class so that the teacher can be sure that the students start out in the right direction, that steps in a process can be discussed, that students can compare their predictions and answers with other students, and so forth. In particular, teachers are encouraged to introduce each new unit and Unit Task in class. Other activities that are recommended for in-class work include

Identifying the Information You Need
Preview the Reading and Previewing Strategy Exercises
Topics for Discussion
Introduction to the Reading Strategies and Strategies for Unknown Vocabulary
Making Connections

A number of the exercise types lend themselves very well to being done as homework activities. These include

Checking Your Comprehension
Exercises practicing Reading Strategies and Strategies for Unknown Vocabulary
Building Your Vocabulary
Writing Your Ideas
Expansion Activities

Using this Book in Different Classes

In Reading Classes This book can serve as the core text in a reading course, with speaking and writing activities based upon it. If a class meets only for an hour at a time, using this text by itself may be sufficient. If a class meets for several hours, the content of this book can be expanded by involving the entire class in some of the Expansion Activities suggested at the end of each unit.

In Writing or Combined Reading/Writing Classes Many writing courses require students to read material that they are then asked to critique or react to in writing. Because of the numerous writing activities built into each reading and each unit, and because of the high-interest readings included here, this text lends itself especially well to such an approach. Although specific, step-by-step writing instruction is not provided in this book, many of the activities ask the student to reflect on written text from both a writer's and a reader's viewpoint. In other words, many of the reading and vocabulary strategy exercises focus students' attention on common writing issues like text organization, main ideas, types of support for arguments, use of examples, use of transition words, common collocations, and so on. Specific writing instruction can easily be added, either through the use of an accompanying writing text, or by supplementing this text with individual writing activities and exercises compiled or developed by the teacher.

TO THE STUDENT

In real life we often need to read for different purposes. We read for different purposes, because we often collect information from many different books, articles, and other sources. Often these books or articles cover topics that are broader than what we need. Therefore, a large part of a reader's job is to discover which articles or parts of articles and books are the most relevant to the topic. It is important to learn to find this information as quickly and easily as possible.

This textbook will introduce you to various skills and strategies that will help you select relevant materials for your topic and accomplish a specific purpose. Along the way, you will also learn skills and strategies for synthesizing information (putting information together from different sources) and presenting your work according to the stated purpose.

HOW YOU CAN BECOME A BETTER READER

Here are several things you can do to help yourself become a better reader in English:

- *Think Before You Read* Think carefully before you read. Don't just start reading. Before you begin, look at what you are reading and try to guess what it is going to be about.

- *Find the General Topic of the Reading* Think about what you already know about this topic. What have you heard about this subject before? Are there any pictures with the text? What are they about? Are any of the objects in the pictures familiar to you? Can you imagine something about this subject in your mind? Bring this information to the front of your mind as you read. Then compare the information in what you are reading to what you already know about the topic.

- *Think about Your Purpose in Reading* Use this purpose to decide if the information is useful, if you need to read more, or if you need to change

the way you are reading. Don't worry if not all of the information is related or useful to your purpose. Don't worry about skipping some parts of the reading if they are not related to the purpose.

- *Don't Worry About Understanding the Exact Meaning of Every Word* Try to get a general idea of the meaning, using any techniques you can. Take a chance and try to be satisfied with a little bit of fuzziness in your understanding of new words. Later, think again about these words and ask yourself if you understand the meaning a little more clearly after having read a text.

- *Read a Passage More Than Once* Sometimes you will notice something the second time that you didn't see the first time. Each time you read, look for more information.

- *Ask Yourself Questions While You Read* Then look for the answers to these questions in the reading. If you can't find the answers, look again, or change your question, and then read again.

- *Question the Author While You Read* In other words, ask questions in your mind as you are reading. Do you agree with the author? Are you surprised by the information? Do you believe what the author is saying? (Remember: Just because it's in print doesn't mean it is necessarily true.)

- *Try to Read as Much as You Can* Find a newspaper, a magazine, or a book in English about something that you are interested in. Read it whenever you have some free time, such as when you are on a bus or waiting for someone. Try to focus on understanding the main ideas, even if you don't understand all of the small details. Don't worry if you don't understand some of the words. Try to use your dictionary as little as possible—or only for the most important words. The most important thing is that you read something you are interested in, and that you continue reading and reading.

Getting Started

What is *reading for a purpose?*

When you read, there is always a reason, that is, a *purpose* for reading. When you read a street sign, a textbook, or a newspaper, you are reading for a particular purpose.

Think about these materials. Why do you read them? Complete the chart below. Then discuss your answers with your classmates.

READING MATERIAL	PURPOSE(S)
1. a map	_____
2. a catalogue	_____
3. an advertisement	_____
4. a textbook	_____
5. a dictionary	_____
6. a postcard	_____
7. a book review	_____

You probably found that you read these materials for different purposes. Some purposes are:

• to learn how to do something

• to complete an assignment

• to study for a test

• to decide if you should buy something

• to enjoy yourself

PREVIEW UNIT

This book will help you improve your reading skills by teaching you how to read different kinds of materials for different purposes. In particular, the objective, or goal, is to help you become a better reader in school, at work or in other situations which often require you to read and understand large amounts of material.

When you are not reading for enjoyment, you often begin with a topic that you need to find information about or a question that you need to answer. Then there are three important steps that good readers use in order to read more efficiently and effectively.

Step 1: Preview

Sometimes when you are reading for a purpose, it is necessary to get information from several different books, articles, and other sources. Therefore, a large part of the job is to discover which articles, or parts of articles and books, are the most relevant to the topic. You need to learn to find this information as quickly and easily as possible. Previewing helps you to do this.

When you preview, you look at an article or text quickly to try to find out if it is likely to give you important information and where in the article you might find it. In this book, you will learn several previewing techniques.

Step 2: Read Closely

Reading closely means paying careful attention when you are reading. You will also learn strategies that will help you increase your understanding when you are reading closely.

Step 3: Note Important Information

After you have read, you must have a way of remembering the important information. This is particularly necessary when you are using several different sources. You will learn a number of different techniques that will help you to do this.

Good readers use different strategies depending on their purpose, the information they need, and the difficulty of the material they are reading. You may not have realized it, but you probably use many reading skills and strategies already.

Look at the list of reading materials again. Do you read them all in the same way? Which ones do you read from start to finish? Which ones do you read only in certain parts? Do you read every word of them? Do you read them slowly or quickly?

READING MATERIAL	HOW DO YOU READ IT?
1. a map	_____
2. a catalogue	_____
3. an advertisement	_____
4. a textbook	_____
5. a dictionary	_____
6. a postcard	_____
7. a book review	_____

When you read in different ways, you are using reading strategies. Let's look at three common ways of reading.

1. Scanning: When we scan, we read quickly, looking for specific information.

Imagine that you want to find the telephone number of a man named Mr. Rounds. You don't know his first name, but you know that he lives on Green Street.

Rounds, Donald	98 High St.	254–0964
Rounds, Edith	109 Maple St.	254–6740
Rounds, Frank	7 Lake Dr.	257–3266
Rounds, Gregory	18 Green St.	258–6873
Rounds, Henry	66 Oak St.	257–1149
Rounds, John	208 Cedar St	254–3864
Rounds, Kenneth	67 Harris Pl	258–8538
Rounds, Marjorie	417 River Rd	257–5922

What answer did you find? How did you find the answer? If you looked for the word "Green" you were probably scanning.

2. Skimming: When we skim, we read quickly to get a general idea of the reading. One common reason for skimming is to get enough information to decide if we want to continue reading further.

Quickly look at this book review. What is the reviewer's opinion of the book? Is it positive or negative?

Carol Macmillan's first novel is called *The Carpenter.* It isn't a perfect novel, but it's close. *The Carpenter* tells the story of a selfish man who learns to help others and, in the end, helps himself. Richard Nelson is a successful accountant with a wife and two children that he rarely sees. His life is an American success story until the day his wife announces that she is leaving him and taking their children with her. Although Richard had little time for his family, he goes into a deep depression and ends up in a mental institution. There he learns carpentry and when he gets out, he decides to work as a carpenter rather than as an accountant. Through this work, he becomes a more complete human being capable of great sympathy and warmth. Ms. Macmillan has created a character and a story that are totally believeable. Although the beginning is a little slow, the pace soon picks up and the book is hard to put down. We'll be looking for more work from this talented young writer.

Were you able to find the reviewer's opinion? Where did you look? What did you look for? Did you find it in less than 15 seconds? If you did, you were probably skimming.

3. Reading closely: When we read closely, we read more slowly and carefully. We read closely when we want to understand as much as possible. We also read this way to be sure that we can find the information we need.

Read the paragraph below and find out the steps for making spaghetti sauce. Then, without looking at the receipe, explain it to a partner.

1. Cut up a small onion and two cloves of garlic.

2. Peel and chop one pound of fresh tomatoes.

3. Put the onion into a frying pan and fry it with a tablespoon of olive oil until it is brown. Then add the garlic and fry for one more minute.

4. Put the chopped tomatoes into the frying pan with the onion and garlic. Fry until the tomatoes are cooked. (About three minutes.)

5. Add some salt and pepper as needed

Were you able to tell your partner the recipe? Were there any parts that you didn't remember? If you could tell your partner the recipe, you probably read the paragraph closely.

Handling Unknown Vocabulary

One of the most difficult problems when you are reading in a foreign language is knowing what to do about the words that you do not understand.

What do you usually do when you are reading and find a word you do not know?

a. I stop and look the word up in a dictionary.

b. I try to guess the general meaning of the word.

c. I skip over the word and continue reading

d. I ask someone the meaning of the word.

Each of these strategies works in some cases. Sometimes, you may decide that having a general idea of the meaning is enough. Other times, you may decide that you can skip over the word and still understand the important ideas in the reading. Occasionally, you may feel that the word is so important that you must stop and look it up in a dictionary. However, in this book you will be learning strategies for dealing with words that you do not understand.

A note about dictionary use: In the beginning, you may feel that you need to use a dictionary often. However, if you practice strategies for handling unknown words in other ways, you will find that you will need to use your dictionary much less over time. You will also find that it is only one of several different strategies you have available to use when you see words that you don't understand.

Developing Your Vocabulary

There are two basic ways of dealing with the problem of new vocabulary in reading. Good readers use both of them. First of all, you can use strategies for handling new words as you read. Second, you can develop your vocabulary as much as possible. As you do this, it is helpful to keep a personal vocabulary list. The more words you know, the fewer you will have to guess the meaning of.

Discuss these questions with your class.

How do you learn new vocabulary?

Where do you find the most useful new words?

Also, much research on reading shows that the best way to develop a powerful vocabulary is to read as much as you can. Even if you do not keep your own personal vocabulary list, the more you read, the more words you will learn.

The Organization of this Text

Look at the Table of Contents of this book. The book is divided into four units. Write their names below.

1. _____

2. _____

3. _____

4. _____

Each unit has one or two Unit Tasks.

5. Which units have two Unit Tasks? _____

6. Which unit has only one? _____

Generally, you will do a Unit Task after you have finished three readings. As you are reading, you will be reminded to look for information related to the Unit Task. Some readings will be directly related to the task. They will give you a lot of helpful information. Others will be related only indirectly. They may give you very little information to help you do the the task. In the end, you will need to put together information from several readings in order to do the Unit Task well. If you would like to do even more reading on a topic, you can find extra readings for each unit in the appendix.

IN THIS UNIT

Reading Strategies

- Understanding how information is organized
- Finding the topic of each paragraph
- Dealing with technical readings
- Identifying the author's purpose
- Making inferences
- Looking for language signals
- Reading spoken language

Strategies for Unknown Vocabulary

- Recognizing titles and names
- Looking for explanations of unknown words
- Understanding familiar words with special meanings
- Using affixes to guess meaning

Who Should Take Care of the Children?

Local Couple Killed in Plane Crash

Plane crash at Metropolitan Airport kills two.

CHICAGO August 15, 1998 — A Hillsboro couple, Victor and Caroline Crowley, were killed late yesterday afternoon in the crash of their private plane while attempting to land at Metropolitan Airport in Chicago during a violent thunderstorm. The reason for the crash has yet to be determined. Mr. Crowley, who had at least ten years of experience flying, was piloting the plane at the time of the crash. Local authorities believe that Mr. Crowley lost control of the plane because of the bad weather. However, Robert Crowley, brother of the victim, said, "My brother was an excellent pilot. He landed safely in much worse weather than this. I believe it was a mechanical problem." The Crowleys were the only two passengers on the plane at the time of the crash. Their two young children, Meredith, 4, and Andrew, 2, are in the care of relatives. The investigation into the plane crash is continuing. Experts hope to release their final report by the end of the week.

Discuss these questions with your classmates.

1. Where is this reading from? How do you know?

   a. a novel   b. a textbook   c. a newspaper

2. What happened?

3. When did it happen?

4. Where did it happen?

5. Who did it happen to?

Most children live with their parents. When one parent dies, the other parent usually takes care of the children. But what happens when both parents die? Who should take care of the children then? How should this decision be made?

There are seven readings in this unit. Each of them represents a different kind of text. Some readings will be fairly easy for you to understand. Other readings may be quite challenging.

Look at each of the readings in the unit. Match the readings in the unit with the types of readings listed below. Write the reading numbers on the lines. How do you know which kind of reading each one is? (Some types of readings appear more than once in this unit.)

READING NUMBER(S)

1. consumer information booklet   _____

2. newspaper article   _____

3. personal letter   _____

4. a legal paper (document)   _____

5. professional report   _____

6. court transcript   _____

7. business letter   _____

PART  READING FOR A PURPOSE

In this unit you are going to think about who takes care of children if their parents cannot. You will read about what the laws say. You will also continue to read about the couple killed in the plane crash. Your purpose in this unit is to find out information about the people involved in this case. You will then use this information to decide who should take care of the children.

Before you read, you will identify the information that you will need for the Unit Task. Then, as you read, you will use the three steps in reading for a purpose that you learned about in "Getting Started" (the Preview Unit). Can you identify the correct order of the steps in the box below?

> Read Closely
> ✓ Identify the Information You Need
> Note Useful Information
> Preview the Reading

Write the names of the steps on the lines on the next page. An example has been done for you.

Pre-step <u>Identify the Information You Need</u> Decide what you are going to look for when you read.

Step 1 _____ Look quickly at a reading to find out if it contains useful information.

Step 2 _____ Read the article.

Step 3 _____ Look back to make notes or underline the information that you need for the Unit Task.

Identify the Information You Need

1. **In order to do the Unit Task, you will need to find out about the parents and what they wanted for their children. You will also need to find out about the people who could take care of the children (or be their guardians). Finally, you will need to find out what the law says. With a classmate, write three sets of questions. An example has been done for you.**

QUESTIONS ABOUT THE PARENTS

1. <u>Did they leave any instructions about who they wanted to take care of the children?</u>

2. _____?

3. _____?

4. _____?

5. _____?

QUESTIONS ABOUT THE PEOPLE WHO COULD TAKE CARE OF THE CHILDREN

6. <u>Who are they?</u>

7. _____?

8. _____?

9. _____?

10. _____?

QUESTIONS ABOUT THE LAW

11. <u>Who does the law say should take care of children who lose their parents?</u>

12. _____?

13. _____?

14. _____?

15. _____?

2. **Compare your questions with your classmates' questions. Are there any questions that you want to add or remove from your list? Copy your final list of questions into your notebook.**

3. **Look ahead to the readings. Which reading or readings will give you the answer to each category of questions? Write the numbers on the lines below.**

QUESTION CATEGORIES	READING NUMBER(S)
1. Questions about the parents	_____
2. Questions about the possible guardians	_____
3. Questions about the law	_____

READING 1: "OBITUARIES AND FUNERALS"

Step 1: Preview the Reading

THE IMPORTANCE OF PREVIEWING

Previewing a reading is important for several reasons:

- It helps you understand how information is presented in the reading. This information will help you read better because it will help you prepare for or guess what is coming next.

- It gives information about the content of the reading. Then, you can think about what you already know about this topic (your general knowledge). Combining what you read with what you already know about a topic will help you understand better.

- It helps you decide if this reading will have information that is useful for the Unit Task or purpose.

---

1. **What do you know about this reading before you even read it? (Hint: Where is it from? What kinds of information will it probably contain?)**

2. **Where did you look to find information about the reading?**

3. **Look back at the list of questions you wrote in your notebook in order to do the Unit Task. Which questions might this text answer? Put a check mark (✓) next to those questions.**

Step 2: Read Closely

Read the article and look for the answers to the questions you checked in your notebook. If you find any answers, write them next to your questions.

OBITUARIES AND FUNERALS

Victor Crowley
Caroline (Ames) Crowley

1   Victor Crowley, 38, and his wife Caroline, 36, died Sunday evening in the crash of their private plane while trying to land at Chicago Metropolitan Airport. Mr. Crowley, who was president and founder of Computech, was born at Hillsboro General Hospital on July 12, 1960. He was the son of Henry and Violet (Kingston) Crowley. He graduated from St. Paul's Academy in 1978, and was a 1982 graduate of Notre Dame College in Indiana. After graduating from college, Mr. Crowley worked for the computer software division of IBM in Boston, Massachusetts. There, he met his wife, Caroline Ames. They were married in 1985. He returned to Hillsboro with his wife in 1987 when he started his own software company, Computech.

2   Mr. Crowley was an enthusiastic member and past president of the Hillsboro Aviation Club, as well as member of the Optimists, a businessmen's club which tries to help local youth. He also sat on the local board of the American Aid Society and worked as a volunteer baseball coach for the Youth Baseball League.

3   Caroline Crowley was born in Tacoma, Washington, on November 18, 1961. She was the daughter of Bennet and Ruth (McCawley) Ames. She graduated from Tacoma South High School in 1980 and Boston College in 1984. After she graduated from college, she worked as an assistant curator for the Boston Museum of Art. She and Victor Crowley were married in August of 1985.

4   Mrs. Crowley was involved in many local activities. She was a member and past president of the Hillsboro Art Society. In addition, in 1990, she was the first coordinator of the Art Society Fund Drive, which gives money for art projects in the public schools and provides scholarships for art students. She was also the chairperson of City to Country, a group which sends inner-city children to stay with local families in the summer. Mrs. Crowley was also a great music lover. She was an excellent musician and played violin in the Hillsboro Chamber Orchestra from 1988 until her death.

5   Mr. and Mrs. Crowley leave a daughter, Meredith, 4, and a son, Andrew, 2. In addition to his parents, Henry and Violet Crowley of Hillsboro, Mr. Crowley also leaves a brother, Robert Crowley of Chicago, a former sister-in-law, Rebecca Crowley of Milwaukee, Wisconsin, and a nephew, Stephen Crowley, also of Milwaukee. Mrs. Crowley leaves her parents, Bennet and Ruth Ames of Tacoma, Washington, and a sister and brother-in-law, Karen and Michael Wang of Seattle, Washington.

6   Calling hours will take place in the Alstead Funeral Home on Tuesday from 7 to 9 p.m. A funeral mass will be celebrated by Father John Cooper on Wednesday, August 17th at 10:30, at St. Peter's Church. The burial will be in Pine Grove Cemetery.

7   Memorial contributions may be made to: The Optimists Club of Hillsboro and the Art Society Fund Drive.

1. **Look back at Reading 1 to find the information to complete this time line for Victor Crowley's life. An example has been done for you.**

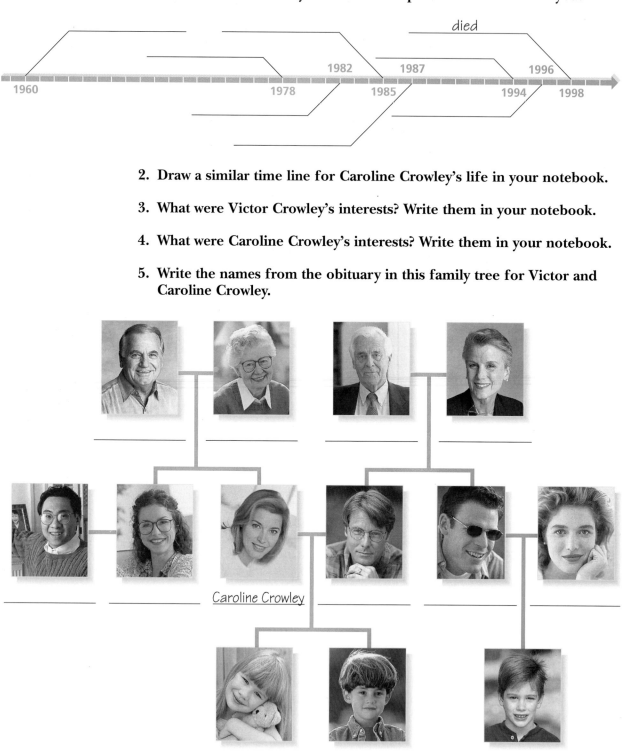

died

1960   1978   1982   1985   1987   1994   1996   1998

2. **Draw a similar time line for Caroline Crowley's life in your notebook.**

3. **What were Victor Crowley's interests? Write them in your notebook.**

4. **What were Caroline Crowley's interests? Write them in your notebook.**

5. **Write the names from the obituary in this family tree for Victor and Caroline Crowley.**

Caroline Crowley

B. Topics for Discussion

Discuss the following questions with your classmates.

1. What kind of people do you think the Crowleys were? Why?

2. What is an obituary? What is its purpose? Do newspapers in your country print obituaries? Are they similar to or different from this obituary? In what ways?

C. Reading Strategies

READING STRATEGY:
Understanding How Information is Organized

Every well-written text has a definite organization. As a reader, it is your job to figure out what that organization is. When you know the organization, you can predict what is coming as you read. Here are three common types of organization:

Chronological Order   Puts events in time order

Description   Describes a person, place, thing, or idea

Comparison/Contrast   Explains how two things are the same or different

Each type of organization presents information in a specific way. However, it is not uncommon to have more than one type of organization in the same text.

An obituary often has two of the above kinds of organization. Which two do you think they are? Why?

---

1. **Look at these words or characteristics. Which ones might you find in each type of organization? Check (✓) the correct column(s). An example has been done for you.**

	Description	Chronological order	Comparison/contrast
1. dates	✓	✓	✓
2. words such as *both, neither, also, similar, different, the same, as...as*			
3. the words *before, after, then, when*			
4. many adjectives			
5. stative verbs such as *have, look like, weigh, believe, know, contain, like, smell, want,* etc.			

2. **Look quickly at the reading. Draw a vertical line (|) on the left side next to the paragraphs about Victor Crowley. Draw two vertical lines (| |) next to the paragraphs about Caroline Crowley. How are these paragraphs organized?**

READING STRATEGY: Finding the Topic of Each Paragraph

Just as a reading has a topic, each paragraph in a reading usually has one main topic. All of the sentences in that paragraph present information related to that topic. For example, paragraph 1 is about Victor Crowley's life. All of the sentences explain the important things that happened in his life.

What is paragraph 2 about?

---

3. **Complete this diagram of the reading. Each box describes one paragraph. An example has been done for you.**

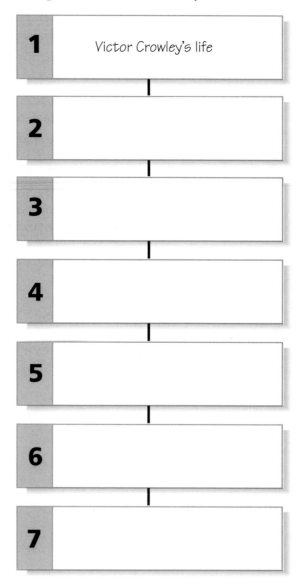

1   Victor Crowley's life

2

3

4

5

6

7

D. Strategies for Unknown Vocabulary

When you read, you may see words that you do not know. Sometimes these words are titles or names. Look at this sentence:

He graduated from St. Paul's Academy.

What is the easiest way to recognize a title or a name?

1. Look back at Reading 1. The names of several organizations and businesses are mentioned. Find five of them and write them below.

1. _Computech_____

2. _____

3. _____

4. _____

5. _____

Sometimes a writer explains an unknown word for the reader. This is especially true for technical vocabulary, titles and names which cannot be found in a dictionary. The explanation often comes right after the word. Sometimes, however, it may come before the word.

Look at this example:

...the Optimists, <u>a businessmen's club which tries to help local youth</u>.

Can you tell what the Optimists do?

2. Which of these organizations are explained in the reading? Write the explanations you find on the lines.

1. Art Society Fund Drive _____

_____

2. Hillsboro Chamber Orchestra _____

_____

3. City to Country _____

_____

4. Boston Museum of Art _____

_____

5. Computech _____

_____

Sometimes a reading contains a word that you know but the meaning is a little different.

Look at this sentence:

He also **sat** on the local board of the American Aid Society and worked as a volunteer baseball coach for the Youth Baseball League.

Does the word **sat** have its usual meaning here?

If not, can you use the meaning that you know to help you understand the meaning here?

How would you explain this meaning of **sat**?

3. **Look at paragraph 6. What familiar word is used in a different way? How would you explain its meaning here? Write the word and its meaning on the line.**

Step 3: Note Useful Information

1. **Look back at the questions you wrote in your notebook that you thought this reading might answer. Did you find the answers when you read it? Did it give you any information about other questions?**

2. **Copy these boxes into your notebook. Write the information that you feel is important to remember from this reading. In order to decide which information is important, you will have to think about the Unit Task and your purpose for reading. Remember: Your purpose is to find information that will help you decide who should take care of the Crowleys' children.**

IMPORTANT INFORMATION ABOUT CAROLINE CROWLEY

IMPORTANT INFORMATION ABOUT VICTOR CROWLEY

E. Building Your Vocabulary

Use these steps to build your vocabulary with words from the reading.

1. Look back at Reading 1. Make a list of five to ten words that were new for you. Use these guidelines:

   • Choose words that you think will be important when you do the Unit Task.

   • Choose words that seem generally useful.

2. Write these words in your personal vocabulary list. Then, copy the sentence or phrase where you found each one and write the meaning in your own words, including the part of speech. If you are still unsure of the meaning, look it up in a dictionary and write the meaning in your own words in your vocabulary notebook.

3. Check (✓) the words in your list that you think will be important for the Unit Task.

F. Writing Your Ideas

Look at the writing topics below. Choose at least one and write about it.

1. Imagine the kind of life that Victor and Caroline Crowley lived. Write an essay in which you describe their lives. Give as many details as possible. Be careful that your details fit the information you found in Reading 1.

2. Would you have liked the Crowleys? Would you have had interests in common with them? Why or why not? Explain your reasons.

READING 2: "NOMINATION OF GUARDIAN"

Step 1: Preview the Reading

1. **What kind of reading is this? Why do you think so?**

2. **What kind of language do you think this reading will contain? Why?**

3. **What useful information do you expect to learn from this document?**

4. **Look back at the list of questions you wrote in your notebook for the Unit Task. Which questions might this text answer? Put a check mark (✓) next to them.**

Legal documents often have a lot of technical language which is difficult even for native speakers to understand. Therefore, when you read this legal document, remember your purpose and try to get the main idea without spending a lot of time trying to understand all of the words. (Of course, if you ever have to sign a legal document, you may want to ask a lawyer to explain it to you before you sign it.)

Read the document and look for the answers to the questions you checked in your notebook. Write any answers that you find next to your questions.

READING 2

S.T. Banks and Partners
Attorneys at Law • 327 Maple St. • Hillsboro, IL 60713

Nomination of Guardian

We, Victor and Caroline Crowley, hereby nominate Robert and Rebecca Crowley to be the legal guardians of our daughter Meredith Crowley. We believe that they will be able to provide a secure, stable, loving home for our daughter in the event of our deaths. We hereby swear that this declaration is made voluntarily and represents our true intention.

Hillsboro, Illinois
place

April 17, 1994
date

Victor Crowley
Victor Crowley

Caroline Crowley
Caroline Crowley

Witnessed by

Angela Medina
Angela Medina

Kevin Payton
Kevin Payton

David Zamora
David Zamora
Notary Public

A. Checking Your Comprehension

Answer these questions about the reading on the lines below.

1. A special legal paper is often called a *document*. Who probably wrote this document?

    _____

2. What is the purpose of this document?

    _____

3. What were Victor and Caroline Crowley's wishes in 1994? Should the authorities follow the parents' wishes when deciding who should have custody of the children?

    _____

B. Topics for Discussion

Discuss the following questions with your classmates.

1. There is someone in the Crowley family who is not mentioned in this document. Who is it? Why was the person left out?

2. Are the parents' wishes important in a case such as this?

3. Do you think they chose the right guardian?

4. Do you have any reason to believe that Victor and Caroline Crowley's choice changed after 1994? Explain.

C. Reading Strategies

_____

READING STRATEGY: Dealing with Technical Readings

When a text has a lot of technical or specialized vocabulary, it helps to read it in a different way from other texts. First of all, you may find a lot of words and phrases that are unfamiliar. This is particularly true in legal documents where technical, legal words may be used instead of everyday language.

When you read a document that has a lot of technical language, try not to be frustrated by the words that you do not understand. Read to get a general idea of the meaning and do not worry about the details.

_____

Look back at Reading 2. Cross out the words that you can ignore for now. Compare your work with a classmate's. Did you cross out the same words?

Step 3: Note Useful Information

Did you learn any new information about the Crowleys' wishes for their children? What was it? Add this information to the list of questions and answers in your notebook.

D. Building Your Vocabulary

Use these steps to build your vocabulary with words from the reading.

1. When you do the Unit Task, you will need to discuss who should take care of the Crowleys' children. Which of these words and phrases do you think will be important for this discussion? Check (✓) them.

    ____ hereby   ____ legal   ____ secure

    ____ guardian   ____ nominate   ____ stable

    ____ in the event of   ____ nomination   ____ swear

    ____ custody

2. Write into your personal vocabulary list the words that you checked. Then, copy the sentence or phrase where the words appear in the reading and write the meaning in your own words, including the part of speech. If you are still unsure of the meaning, look it up in a dictionary and write the meaning in your own words in your vocabulary notebook.

READING 3: "LETTER TO LYDIA"

Step 1: Preview the Reading

1. **What kind of text is this? How do you know?**

2. **Have you ever received one? Have you ever written one?**

3. **What kind of information do you expect to find in this reading?**

4. **Who wrote this text?**

5. **Who received this text?**

6. **What is the relationship between these two people? Why do you think so?**

7. **Look back at the list of questions you wrote in your notebook for the Unit Task. Which questions might this text answer? Put a check mark (✓) next to them.**

Step 2: Read Closely

Starting with this reading, all of the readings will have questions in the left margin. These questions will give you more practice with the Reading Strategies and Strategies for Unknown Vocabulary that you are learning. However, the first time that you read, try to understand the text without reading the margin questions. Take a piece of paper and cover them.

1. **Read the text and look for the answers to the questions you checked in your notebook. If you find any answers, write them next to your questions.**

2. **Read the article a second time. This time, as you read, look at the margin questions and try to answer them. They will help you to find the information that you need for the Unit Task.**

READING 3

C. Crowley
2186 Lincoln Dr.
Hillsboro, IL 60713

VIA AIR MAIL

Ms. Lydia Montgomery
8B Granta Mews
London SW1 England

USA

Dear Lydia,   June 25, 1998

1 I was so glad to get your letter the other day. I always miss talking to you when you are away. I'm sorry to hear that you and Alex have decided to end your engagement. However, I understand how difficult it must be to have a career like yours and a relationship as well. Sometimes even Vic and I do not see each other enough because we have so many different activities – and we live in the same house! It must be impossible to have a relationship when the two of you are on different continents. Of course, I can understand how Alex feels. He wants to have someone with him every day but that just can't be you. You have worked too hard to give up your career now. Maybe the two of you were just not right for each other. Don't worry, Lyd, you'll find someone, I'm sure.

2 Speaking of family matters and relationships, Vic and I have something to ask you. You know we chose his brother, Robert and his sister-in-law Rebecca, to be the kids' legal guardians if anything happened to us. I was never very happy with that decision but Vic insisted, so I finally agreed to sign the document. Well, now as you know, Robert and Rebecca are divorced. Rebecca has moved to Milwaukee with their son Stephen. We no longer think that Robert would be a suitable guardian. There are a couple of reasons for our decision. First of all, he is a bachelor and, by himself, he is just too irresponsible to take care of children. His irresponsibility has also led to serious money problems. He was forced to file for bankruptcy when Communicom failed last year. Even his father refused to help him this time. He loves the kids, I know, but I don't think he would be able to take care of them alone.

3 Our problem is that we can't think of any couple that we would like to name. We were wondering if you would be willing to be Meredith and Andrew's guardian? We know that with your work, it would not be easy. However, if anything happened to us, the children would be millionaires, and money would certainly help solve any of the problems they might have without us.

4 Think about it. Don't decide now. We both love you like a sister. Meredith adores you, too. She's always asking when Aunt Lydia is coming to visit again. And, of course, we're both in perfect health and have no plans to die anytime soon, so you probably will never have to do anything. We can talk when you come to visit in September after your tour. But don't worry if you feel that you have to say no. We will understand.
    I know that you are working, but try to have a great time in Europe anyway!

5 Love, Caroline
    P.S. Meredith has started violin lessons. Her dream is to be just like her Aunt Lydia!

1. Can you guess what *Communicom* is?

2. What does *fail* probably mean here?

3. What is the normal meaning of *name*? What does it mean here?

A. Checking Your Comprehension

Answer these questions about the reading on the lines below.

1. Where was Lydia when she received this letter?

   _____

2. What did Lydia probably tell Caroline in her last letter?

   _____

3. What favor does Caroline ask Lydia to do?

   _____

4. What reasons does she give for this decision?

   _____

B. Topics for Discussion

Discuss the following questions with your classmates.

1. What would you do if you were in Lydia's situation and received a letter like this from a friend? Explain.

2. How would your life change if you received a letter like this, and you agreed to do what it asked? Why?

C. Reading Strategies

READING STRATEGY: Identifying the Author's Purpose

When you are reading, it is important to understand the writer's purpose. For example, if you are reading an advertisement, you know that the writer's purpose is to persuade you to buy something. Therefore, you may not believe all of the things that he or she tells you.

---

1. **What was Caroline's purpose in writing this letter? (Hint: there may be more than one.) Find the specific place or paragraph in the letter that suggests each purpose.**

PURPOSE	LOCATION (PARAGRAPH/LINE)
1. _____	_____
2. _____	_____
3. _____	_____

When we read, we can get information in two different ways. We get some information directly—the writer tells us. We get other information indirectly— that is, we infer it or read between the lines. When we make inferences we depend on our general knowledge of the world.

Read this sentence:

However, if anything happened to us, the children would be millionaires, and money would certainly help solve any of the problems they might have without us.

Can you infer why the children would be millionaires? What do you know about life in general that helped you to answer this question?

2. **Answer these inference questions. Explain which information in the reading helps you to find the answers to each question.**

1. What do you think the problems that Caroline refers to might be?

   _____

2. Are Caroline and Lydia good friends?

   _____

3. What is Lydia's work?

   _____

4. Does Lydia have to travel a lot?

   _____

5. Has Robert Crowley had money problems before? How do you know?

   _____

Step 3: Note Useful Information

In order to do the Unit Task, you will have to compare the people who could be guardians. In your notebook, make a chart like the one below. What names can you put in it? What positive information can you put in the chart? Is there any negative information that you can put in the chart?

Candidates	Relationship to Victor & Caroline Crowley	Positive points	Negative points

D. Building Your Vocabulary

Use these steps to build your vocabulary with words from the reading.

1. Look back at Reading 3. Make a list of five to ten words that were new for you. Use these guidelines:

   - Choose words that you think will be important when you do the Unit Task.

   - Choose words that seem generally useful.

2. Write these words in your personal vocabulary list. Then, copy the sentence or phrase where you found each one and write the meaning in your own words, including the part of speech. If you are still unsure of the meaning, look it up in a dictionary and write the meaning in your own words in your vocabulary notebook.

3. Check (✓) the words that may be important for the Unit Task.

4. When you are learning new words it is important to be aware of word combinations. A word combination is a group of words that often appear together. Two and three word verbs such as *sit down* and *get along with* are examples of word combinations.

   It is a good idea to learn the words in a word combination together. Some common word combinations in this reading are:

   solve a problem   *be happy with*

   Complete these word combinations from the reading. If you can't remember them, look again at the reading.

   1. _____ course   3. file for _____

   2. _____ guardians   4. take _____ of

   Can you find other word combinations in the reading?

E. Writing Your Ideas

Look at the writing topics below. Choose at least one and write about it.

1. Write about a time that you asked a friend to do a big favor for you or a time that a friend asked you to do him or her a favor. What was the favor? What was the answer?

2. How would you feel if friends or relatives asked you to be the legal guardian for their children? Would it make you happy or would it be a problem? Why?

READING 4: "LETTER FROM A LAWYER"

Step 1: Preview the Reading

1. **Compare this reading with Reading 3. Do the two texts look the same? How do they look different?**

2. **Who wrote this text? Who received it? What is the relationship between these people?**

3. **What kind of language do you expect to find in this reading? Why?**

4. **Look back at the questions you wrote in your notebook for the Unit Task. Check (✓) the ones that may be answered in this reading.**

Step 2: Read Closely

1. **Will you read this text in the same way that you read Reading 2 or Reading 3? Why or why not?**

2. **Read the text. The first time you read, remember to cover up the margin questions. Look for the answers to the questions you checked in your notebook. Write them next to your questions.**

3. **Read the text again. Use the margin questions and try to answer them. They will help you find information that you need for the Unit Task.**

READING 4

HOLLIS, COLTRANE & SWEET
Attorneys at Law • 179 Abbey Road • Santa Monica, CA 90401

September 5, 1998

Ms. Lydia Montgomery
8B Granta Mews
London SW1
England

Dear Ms. Montgomery,

1. What is the purpose of this paragraph?

1   I received your fax this morning asking about the legality of your personal communication from the late Caroline Crowley. Let me first express my sympathy on the tragic death of your close friends. I am sure that it must have been a great shock and a loss to you.

2. What does *personal communication* refer to?

2   As to your question about becoming the legal guardian of the children, I have both good and bad news. First of all, it is unfortunate that the Crowleys were never able to sign another Nomination of Guardian, if the one in favor of Mr. Robert Crowley

was never withdrawn. However, it seems unlikely that the court would give him custody because of his divorce and his financial situation.

3. What is the purpose of paragraphs 2 and 3?

3 Even though you are not a blood relative, the court could still consider making you the guardian because of your long relationship with the Crowleys. However, there are several problems. For one, even though Caroline states that Victor Crowley agreed with her, he didn't sign the letter and that could cause a problem. This may not be so problematic if they discussed changing their nomination of guardian with their own lawyer because then he or she would be able to testify to that fact. Another difficulty may be Victor Crowley's parents. If, as you say, they plan to try to obtain custody, they may have a strong case, especially since they are taking care of the children at the moment.

4. What is the purpose of paragraph 4?

4 If you are truly interested in applying for custody of these children, I suggest that you return to the United States as soon as possible in order to be available to meet with social workers and other court officials who will want to speak with you. However, as your lawyer and your friend, I caution you to think very carefully about this decision. In order to be seen as a suitable guardian, you will have to make many changes in your life. These changes might be a great sacrifice for an accomplished musician such as yourself.

5 If, despite all that I have said, you decide to petition for guardianship, we will, of course, be happy to represent you.

Sincerely yours,

Arlen Coltrane

Arlen Coltrane

A. Checking Your Comprehension

Answer these questions about the reading on the lines below.

1. What good news does the lawyer give Lydia?

   _____

2. What bad news does the lawyer give Lydia?

   _____

3. Does the lawyer think that Robert Crowley will be given custody of the children? Why or why not?

   _____

4. What advice does he give Lydia?

   _____

B. Making Inferences

What inferences can you make about the reading? Answer these questions.

1. Who will decide on this issue? How will the decision be made?

2. Does the lawyer think that Lydia should apply for guardianship?

3. What changes might Lydia have to make in her life?

C. Topics for Discussion

Discuss the following questions with your classmates.

1. What would you do if you were Lydia?

2. What complications does this letter add to Caroline's request?

D. Reading Strategies

READING STRATEGY: Looking for Language Signals

As you are reading, look for "language signals" that tell you what is coming next. These signals often point out important information, and help you to figure out the organization of the reading.

Here is one example of a language signal. What does it tell you to start looking for in the text?

As to your question about becoming the legal guardian of the children, I have **both good and bad news.**

What does the following signal tell you is coming?

First of all, it is unfortunate...

Some signals are a single word. One common signal word is **however. However** has a meaning similar to **but.**

How can you complete this sentence?

She wanted to go. However, _____.

---

1. **Look at these sentences. Underline the language signals and explain what kind of information may follow.**

   1. Victor Crowley agreed with his wife; unfortunately, he...

   2. It will be difficult for Lydia to get custody of the children. The court generally does not like to award custody to non-family members. In addition...

   3. Victor Crowley's parents have a good chance of getting the children. Similarly, Caroline's sister...

   4. The court sometimes gives the children to a non-family member. For example...

2. **Find three places in Reading 4 where *however* is used. What two things is the writer contrasting in each case?**

VOCABULARY STRATEGY: Using Affixes to Guess Meaning

One important way of figuring out the meaning of unknown words is by looking at affixes. There are two kinds of affixes: prefixes and suffixes. Prefixes are added to the beginning of words (for example, **happy—unhappy**). Suffixes are added to the ends of words (for example, **happy—happiness**).

In general, prefixes change the meaning of a word and suffixes may change the part of speech.

How does **un-** change the meaning of **happy**?

What part of speech is **happy**? What part of speech is **happiness**?

Look for these words in the reading. Underline the prefix or the suffix. Circle the root word. Write a definition in your own words on the lines.

1. unfortunate _____

2. unlikely _____

3. problematic _____

4. legality _____

5. guardian _____

Step 3: Note Useful Information

Did this reading give you the information about the candidates that you expected? Put any new information into the chart in your notebook.

F. Building Your Vocabulary

Use these steps to build your vocabulary with words from the reading.

1. Look back at Reading 4. Choose five new words to add to your personal vocabulary list. Remember to look for words that will be useful in discussing the Unit Task. You should also look for words that you think will be generally useful. Write these words in your vocabulary notebook. Then, copy a sentence or phrase where you found each one and write the meaning in your own words, including the part of speech. If you are still unsure of the meaning, look it up in a dictionary and write the meaning in your own words in your vocabulary notebook.

2. Check (✓) the words in your list that you think will be important for the Unit Task.

3. Look for the words in Reading 4 that complete these word combinations:

    1. _____ available to

    2. in _____ of

    3. first _____ all

    4. financial _____

G. Writing Your Ideas

Look at the writing topics below. Choose at least one and write about it.

1. Write the fax that you think Lydia might have sent to her lawyer before he wrote this answer.

2. Rewrite the lawyer's letter to Lydia replacing the legal language with everyday language.

READING 5: "CHOOSING A GUARDIAN FOR YOUR CHILDREN"

Step 1: Preview the Reading

1. What kind of document is this?

2. What do you notice about the format of this document (the way the text is printed or how the text looks)?

PREVIEWING STRATEGY: Scanning

Scanning is a way of reading. When you scan, you look quickly at a text to find specific words and phrases. If you scan a reading to find key words or phrases closely related to your purpose, it can help you decide if you should read the text again closely.

---

3. Scan the list in Reading 5.

1. How many items are there? _____

2. What is it a list of? _____

4. Will this reading answer any of your questions about the people in the case? Might it still be helpful? How?

5. Look back at the questions you wrote in your notebook for the Unit Task. Check (✓) the ones that may be answered in this reading.

Step 2: Read Closely

1. **Read the text. The first time you read, remember to cover up the margin questions. Look for the answers to the questions you checked in your notebook. Write any answers that you find next to your questions.**

2. **Read the text again. Use the margin questions and try to answer them. They will help you to find the information that you need for the Unit Task.**

READING 5

1. What is the topic of this paragraph?

2. What is a *Nomination of Guardian?*

3. How is the rest of the reading organized?

Choosing a Guardian for Your Children

1   All parents worry about what will happen to their children if they (the parents) die. According to the law, if one parent dies or is unable to take care of the children, then the other parent will take over. If both parents die, then the court will appoint a legal guardian for the children.

2   The court first considers the wishes of the parents. Therefore, it is best to name the person you desire to have custody of your children in a written Nomination of Guardian. This is a legal document that your lawyer can write for you. The court must appoint the person named in a Nomination of Guardian unless it is not in the best interests of the child.

3   Of course, it is very important to think carefully about who would be the best guardian for your children. Here are some questions to consider:

Health and Age

- Will this person be able to take care of your children until they are 18 or 21? If he or she is too old, this may not be possible. That is why you should think twice before naming your own parents to be your children's guardians.

- Does this person have health problems that will make it difficult to be a parent? In addition to diseases, think about over-all fitness. Taking care of young children is a lot of work. Someone who doesn't have a lot of energy may find it very difficult.

Relationship

- Do the child and the nominated guardian know each other well? The death of a parent is probably the most difficult

thing for a child to deal with. If they know and like the guardian, it will be easier for them to deal with.

- Are the child and the nominated guardian comfortable with each other?

Experience

- Does the nominated guardian have experience raising children? Your prospective guardian may be wonderful with your child when he or she comes to visit, but raising children is a full-time job. Think carefully before you nominate anyone who has not had children of their own.

- If the answer is yes, how is the relationship between the nominated guardian and his or her own children?

Stability and Security

- Will your nominee be able to give your child a stable, secure and loving environment? Uncle Bill, who is always lots of fun, may not be able to provide the security that children need.

Religion and Culture

- Is the nominee of the same religion and the same cultural background as your child? If religion has been a big part of your child's upbringing then it is especially crucial that the guardian be able to continue the religious practices that your child is familiar with.

- Does your nominee share many of your values? The nominee cannot be an exact copy of you, but your child will have many more adjustment problems if the nominee's basic beliefs are very different from yours.

Time

- Will your nominee be able to spend sufficient time with your child/children? Being a parent is more than just making sure that the children are safe and healthy. It is also going to parent-teacher conferences, baseball practice, dance recitals, etc.

Number of Children

- If you have more than one child, will this person be able to care for all of them? Dividing children among two or more guardians is not a good idea.

Practical Considerations

- What changes will the guardian have to make in order to take care of your child or children? Is your nominee used to taking vacations whenever she wants? Does he expect to keep his house in tip-top order all of the time? Is he or she expected to work long hours and/or weekends? Perhaps the changes he or she has to make will be too much to handle.

- Does he or she have a large enough house?

- Will she have to make special childcare arrangements in order to be able to work? What kinds of arrangements will he be able to make? Does she work at a company that is "child-friendly"?

Finances

- Does the nominee have enough money to care for your child? This is one of the most crucial questions. Having a child can be very expensive, from child-care costs, through ballet and piano lessons, braces and college tuition. Make sure that you have provided as well as you can for your child's future if you cannot be there.

- If the child is provided for in your will or by life insurance, will the nominee use the money responsibly? If you aren't sure, consider nominating a different person to administer the money.

Willingness

- Is your nominee willing to care for your child/children? Even the most supportive and caring friend or relative may have good reasons for not wanting to take on this responsibility.

- You should also nominate alternate choices for guardianship, in case your first nominee is later unable to take your children.

A. Checking Your Comprehension

Look back at the reading for the list of things to think about when choosing a nominee. Use this list to write a description of a "perfect" nominee in your notebook.

B. Topics for Discussion

Discuss the following questions with your classmates.

1. Are there any things that you think should be in this list but are not?

2. Are there any things in this list that you feel are less important than others?

C. Strategies for Unknown Vocabulary

VOCABULARY STRATEGY: More Practice with Affixes

There are two kinds of affixes: prefixes and suffixes. Prefixes are added to the beginning of words. They usually change the meaning of a word. For example, the prefix **il-** changes the word **legal** to its opposite, **illegal.** Both **legal** and **illegal** are adjectives.

Suffixes are added to the ends of words. They usually change the part of speech of a word. For example, the suffix **-er** changes the verb **teach** to the noun **teacher.**

Look for words in the reading that are related to the words below. Complete the chart. How does this help you to guess the meaning? An example has been done for you.

	Your definition	Part of speech	Affix	Related word(s)	Part of speech
1. nominate	to suggest someone to run for an office	verb	-tion	nomination	noun
2. support					
3. responsible					
4. able					
5. stable					
6. secure					
7. health					
8. willing					
9. culture					
10. adjust					

Step 3: Note Useful Information

Did Reading 5 give you more ideas on what to look for in a guardian? If so, use the information to revise the list of questions you wrote in your notebook from page 5.

D. Building Your Vocabulary

Use these steps to build your vocabulary with words from the reading.

1. Look back at the booklet (Reading 5). Choose five new words to add to your personal vocabulary list. Choose the words that you think will be the most useful in discussing the Unit Tasks. You should also choose words that you think will be generally useful. Write these words in your vocabulary notebook. Then, copy a sentence or phrase where you found each one and write the meaning in your own words, including the part of speech. If you are still unsure of the meaning, look it up in a dictionary and write the meaning in your own words in your vocabulary notebook.

2. Check (✓) the words in your list that you think will be important for the Unit Task.

E. Writing Your Ideas

Look at the writing topics below. Choose at least one and write about it.

1. Choose three items from the list in the reading that you think are the most important and explain why.

2. Imagine that you are going to nominate a legal guardian for your children. Who would you nominate and why?

READING 6: "SOCIAL WORKER'S REPORT"

Step 1: Preview the Reading

1. **What are these two texts? How do you know?**

2. **Scan the first page of this report to find the following information. Circle or highlight it.**

   a. reason for the report

   b. who wrote the report

   c. who the report is about

3. **Look back at the questions you wrote in your notebook for the Unit Task. Check (✓) the ones that may be answered in this report. Are there any other questions you would like to add?**

Step 2: Read Closely

1. Read the texts. The first time you read, remember to cover up the margin questions. Look for the answers to the questions you checked in your notebook. Write any answers next to your questions.

2. Read the texts again. Use the margin questions in Reading 6B and try to answer them. They will help you to find the information that you need for the Unit Task.

READING 6A

HILLSBORO FAMILY COURT ⚖
Family Background Report

Date of Investigation: December 8, 1998

Investigator: Deborah Shumann, MSW

Reason for Investigation: petition for guardianship of minors

Minors: Meredith Louise Crowley (4)

Andrew Robert Crowley (2)

Parents: Victor George Crowley (deceased)

Caroline Marie Crowley (née Ames) (deceased)

Person(s) Investigated: Henry and Violet Crowley

Address: 78 Whispering Leaves Lane, Hillsboro, Illinois

Relationship to the minors: Paternal grandparents

READING 6B

1. Who is *I* in this reading?

2. What is the meaning of *sit* here?

3. How is this text organized?

1 I visited the Crowleys in their home on December 8th. Mr. Crowley is retired and no longer directly manages Crowley Engineering. However, he still sits on the board of directors. Mrs. Crowley is a homemaker. Both Mr. and Mrs. Crowley demonstrate a genuine interest in raising their grandchildren. Indeed, the children have been staying with them since the death of their parents in August. Mr. and Mrs. Crowley seem to have a warm, loving, relationship with them. Both children seem happy and well-adjusted. Reports from Meredith's teachers say that after an understandable period of difficulty, she seems to have adjusted to her new situation.

4. What does *in addition* signal?

2 The children have been very well provided for by their parent's will, so money is not a problem. In addition, I think that it is important to note that the Crowleys are well-off, so if they were nominated there would be no question of mismanagement of funds.

5. What does *although* signal?

6. Who is Dr. Rebecca Briscoe?

3 The obvious negative is their ages. Mr. Crowley is 68 and Mrs. Crowley is 66. Although they are still both active and fairly healthy, there is some question about how long they will remain so. Mrs. Crowley has recently been under a doctor's care for arthritis, a condition which, if it gets worse, could make it very difficult for her to care for young children. Mr. Crowley had a heart attack ten years ago; he has had no problems since that time. I have spoken to Dr. Rebecca Briscoe, his cardiologist, and she says that he can have a normally active life.

7. What does *another* signal?

4 Another negative factor is that of values. Mr. Crowley and his son, Victor had some very public disagreements on the construction of government housing for the poor, when Henry Crowley was a member of the town council. In fact, at one point Victor Crowley was the head of Fair Housing, an organization which actively demonstrated against policies of the town council. The elder Mr. Crowley says that these disagreements were worked out long ago; however, some of Victor Crowley's friends do not agree. In fact, they claim that Victor Crowley was helping to organize a demonstration against the employment policies of Crowley Engineering. Henry Crowley says that he had not heard anything of his son's plans.

8. What does *however* signal?

5 Mrs. Violet Crowley is a Roman Catholic and her religion is very important to her. She says that if she and her husband are selected they will send the children to Catholic schools. Victor and Caroline Crowley were Catholic and themselves graduates of Catholic schools; however, they were not regular churchgoers. Interviews with their friends show that they did not want their children to attend religious schools.

A. Checking Your Comprehension

Imagine that you are the social worker. Complete the following form using information from the report (Reading 6B).

Nominee: Henry Crowley

1. Age: _____

2. Occupation: _____

3. Health Status: _____

4. Financial Status: _____

5. Activities/Interests: _____

Nominee: Violet Crowley

1. Age: _____

2. Occupation: _____

3. Health Status: _____

4. Financial Status: _____

5. Activities/Interests: _____

B. Making Inferences

What inferences can you make about the reading? Answer the questions below.

1. Do you think that the social worker believes that the Crowleys would be suitable guardians?

2. Does the social worker think that the Crowleys have been totally honest with her? Why or why not?

C. Topics for Discussion

Discuss the following questions with your classmates.

1. Is there any information that the social worker did not find out that you would like to know about?

2. How would you feel if you had to evaluate people as this social worker does? Would you be able to do this kind of work? Why or why not?

3. How important do you feel it is that the parents' wishes about the education of their children be followed?

READING STRATEGY: More Practice with Paragraph Topics

In a well-organized text each paragraph usually has one main topic. All the sentences in the paragraph give the reader more information about that topic.

---

1. **Complete the boxes with the topic of each paragraph of Reading 6B. An example has been done for you.**

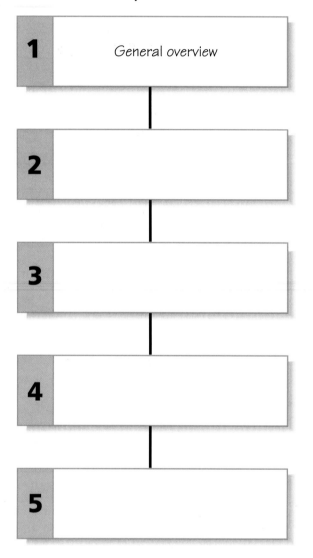

1 | General overview

2 |

3 |

4 |

5 |

2. **Something seems to be missing from the end of the report. What do you think it is?**

VOCABULARY STRATEGY: More Practice with Affixes

What can you remember about affixes? Can you complete these definitions?

A _____ comes at the beginning of a word. It usually changes the meaning of a word. It doesn't change the part of speech.

A _____ comes at the end of the a word. It usually changes the part of speech.

All of the words below are in the reading. Find another related word that is also in the reading. An example has been done for you.

	Your definition	Part of speech	Affix	Related word(s)	Part of speech
1. adjusted	changed in your way of living or thinking in a new situation	adjective	-ment	adjustment	noun
2. manages					
3. agree					
4. organize					
5. demonstrate					
6. religion					

Step 3: Note Useful Information

Look at the chart of possible guardians that you drew into your notebook from page 19. Add the positive and negative information that you have learned about Henry and Violet Crowley.

F. Building Your Vocabulary

Use these steps to build your vocabulary with words from the reading.

1. Look back at the report. Choose five new words to add to your personal vocabulary list. Choose words that you think will be the most useful in discussing the Unit Task. You should also choose words that you think will be generally useful. Write these words in your vocabulary notebook. Then, copy a sentence or phrase where you found each one and write the meaning in your own words, including the part of speech. If you are still unsure of the meaning, look it up in a dictionary and write the meaning in your own words in your vocabulary notebook.

2. Check (✓) the words in your list that you think will be important for the Unit Task.

G. Writing Your Ideas

Look at the writing topics below. Choose at least one and write about it.

1. Imagine that you are the social worker. Write the concluding paragraph to the report.

2. Do you think older people can be good parents or guardians for young children? Why or why not? Explain.

READING 7: "COURT TESTIMONY"

Step 1: Preview the Reading

1. **Scan readings 7A and 7B to answer the following questions:**

   1. What is the purpose of each reading?

   2. What is the connection between the two readings?

2. **Which possible guardians are you likely to get information about in these readings? Also, look back at the questions you wrote in your notebook for the Unit Task. Check (✓) the ones that may be answered in these readings.**

1. **Read the documents.** The first time you read Reading 7B, remember to cover up the margin questions. Look for the answers to the questions you checked in your notebook. Write any answers that you find next to your questions.

2. **Read the documents again.** Use the margin questions in Reading 7B and try to answer them. They will help you to find the information that you need for the Unit Task.

READING 7A

HILLSBORO FAMILY COURT ⚖
HILLSBORO, ILLINOIS

January 23, 1999

This is official notice that a hearing to decide on the guardianship of the minors Meredith and Andrew Crowley, children of the late Victor and Caroline Crowley, will be held in Family Court on February 24th, 1999. The following petitioners, or their legal representatives, are required to be in attendance.

Robert Graham Crowley	Henry David Crowley
Karen Anne Wang	Violet Agnes Crowley
Michael James Wang	Lydia Margaret Montgomery

Any petitioner who does not attend or send a legal representative will not be considered for guardianship.

*HILLSBORO, ILLINOIS
CLERK OF COURTS
JEFFERSON COUNTY*

READING 7B

HILLSBORO FAMILY COURT ⚖
HILLSBORO, ILLINOIS

JUDGE LOUISE ACKERMAN
CASE #8732
              February 24, 1999
    T R A N S C R I P T   O F   H E A R I N G
       —   —   —

1   JUDGE ACKERMAN: Now can you tell me, in your own words, Mrs. Wang, why you believe that you should be nominated as guardian?
       —   —   —

2   KAREN WANG: Yes, I can, your honor. My husband Mike and I have been married for 12 years. We umm, we love children and we would be able to provide a good home for both Meredith and Andrew, so it would, it would be a… a blessing to have Merry and Andrew because we have um… We have never had children of our own. It's not that we didn't want children. We really love kids and couldn't wait to have our own but it just… it just

1. Who does *your honor* refer to?

2. What is Meredith's nickname?

didn't happen. Mike, my husband and I, we're both teachers. He teaches in an elementary school and I'm working in a high school right now. We're not rich, but we're doing okay. We live in a nice house in a good neighborhood and the house is large enough for the children. Each of them can have their own rooms. There are plenty of kids in the neighborhood, so they'd have lots of friends. I just think we could give them a good life. We'd be good parents, I'm sure. If we become Meredith and Andrew's parents, umm I mean guardians, I'll have to quit my job. I know it's important for kids to have a full-time mother. Not that I think that women shouldn't work, but if you can, you should stay home with your children when they're young. I know my sister Caroline thought so too. That's why she quit working when Merry was born.

— — —

3 JUDGE ACKERMAN: Do you have any idea why your sister and brother-in-law did not nominate you and your husband to be guardians in the first place?

— — —

4 KAREN WANG: Yes, I do, your honor. It is difficult to admit this now that she is gone, but my sister Caroline and I never got along very well. The truth is that I was always jealous of her. She had so much, your honor. I mean, she was talented and smart and pretty. It sounds pretty dumb now but I always thought my parents liked her best. You know how it is with sisters… really, growing up, it was difficult to be Caroline's older sister. She was always winning prizes and getting on the honor roll at school and performing in public and getting to be queen of the senior prom – stuff like that. I was green with envy and my jealousy caused a lot of problems between us. Now that… that she is gone, I wish I could talk to her again for just five minutes so I could tell her how sorry I am for everything and… I'm sorry, your honor. This is very upsetting for me. You need to understand, that… that one reason I would like to take care of Meredith and Andrew is to try to make up to Caroline for all the problems between us. I hope that I can get to know her, by taking care of her children.

3. What does *in the first place* mean?

4. What reasons does Karen Wang give for being jealous of her sister?

5   JUDGE ACKERMAN: I see. Well now, you don't live in Hillsboro. All the children's relationships are here. What would you do about that?

—   —   —   —

6   KAREN WANG: Well, we would be willing to bring the children here to visit several times a year. They could even come and spend the summers with their grandparents. And, of course, the Crowleys would always be welcome in our home. And if the court thought it would be best, we would even be willing to move out here to Hillsboro. I mean, I'm sure that Mike could find a job. He's a great teacher and they're always looking for men to teach elementary school.

—   —   —   —

7   JUDGE ACKERMAN: As you mentioned, you have no children of your own. Suddenly having to take care of two young children could be quite difficult. Can you tell me what experience you have with young children?

—   —   —   —

8   KAREN WANG: Well, of course in our jobs we have to deal with children all of the time. As I said, Mike works in an elementary school. He's great with kids. They all love him. In the summers he always works as a volunteer baseball coach. When he and my brother-in-law Victor got together they always talked about baseball. And well, I teach music in high school, but I used to teach in elementary school, so I have worked with young children too. Also, Mike has ten nieces and nephews who all live near us. We're always visiting back and forth. In fact, his sister, Gloria, and her husband often leave their three children with us when they can't umm… find a sitter. So, we actually spend a lot of time with young kids.

5. What is a *sitter?*

A. Checking Your Comprehension

Answer these questions about the reading on the lines below.

1. What is Karen and Michael Wang's financial situation?

2. How was Karen's relationship with her sister?

3. What reason does Karen give for wanting to be the guardian of her niece and nephew?

4. What evidence does Karen give that she and her husband would be able to take care of the children?

B. Making Inferences

What inferences can you make about the reading? Answer the questions below.

1. Do you think that Karen Wang answered the judge's questions truthfully? Why or why not?

2. Do you think that Karen and Michael Wang like children? Why?

3. Do you think that Karen and Caroline had any other brothers or sisters?

C. Topics for Discussion

Discuss the following questions with your classmates.

1. What kind of person do you think Karen Wang is?

2. Are there any other questions that the judge should have asked?

3. Do you think that the judge believes Karen?

D. Reading Strategies

READING STRATEGY: Reading Spoken Language

A transcript is a written report of a person's exact words. Reading spoken language is different from reading written language. It can be more difficult. Spoken language is often not as well-organized as written language. Spoken language also often contains incomplete sentences and short phrases connected by words such as **and, but** or **so.** When people speak, they often use different words and phrases than they do when they write. Spoken language is usually less formal. Below are some examples:

formal	informal
children	kids
mother	mom
receive	get

Look at the quotes below. What do you see that would not occur in written language?

She was always winning prizes and getting on the honor roll at school and performing in public and getting to be queen of the senior prom—stuff like that.

Mike, my husband and I, we're both teachers.

---

1. **Look at the transcript. Underline five places in the text that show that this text is someone's exact words.**

2. **Choose three of the sections that you found and rewrite them in a more formal writing style.**

E. Building Your Vocabulary

Use these steps to build your vocabulary with words from the reading.

1. Look back at the reading. Choose five new words to add to your personal vocabulary list. Choose words that you think will be the most useful in discussing the Unit Task. You should also choose words that you think will be generally useful. Write these words in your vocabulary notebook. Then, copy a sentence or phrase where you found each one and write the meaning in your own words, including the part of speech. If you are still unsure of the meaning, look it up in a dictionary and write the meaning in your own words in your vocabulary notebook.

2. Check (✓) the words in your list that you think will be important for the Unit Task.

Look at the vocabulary list you have written for this unit. On another sheet of paper, copy down all of the words that have a check mark after them. Then copy down all of the words that are related (e.g. *nominee, nomination,* etc.). Now, look at the first list and decide if there are any other words that will be important for the Unit Task. Add these words to the second list.

The second list is a list of <u>active vocabulary</u> words. These are the words that you will need to learn to use. The words which appear only on the first list are <u>passive vocabulary</u>. These are words that you should understand when you see them but may not be able to use them yet.

> ### UNIT TASK:
> ### Deciding Who Should Care for the Children
>
> Prepare for a discussion on who should take care of the children. To do this you should review your informational boxes about the parents from page 12 and the charts about the candidates from page 19. In addition, look back at your list of questions from page 5. Are there any that are not answered? If so, look at the readings again. Remember, you may not find all of the information that you were looking for. If you have time, you may also want to read the extra readings at the back of this book.

Complete the following steps to help you do the Unit Task:

1. Choose the candidate or candidates that you think are best. Write three reasons for your choice on the lines below.

Name: _____

    a. _____

    b. _____

    c. _____

2. Write the reasons why each of the other people is not as good a candidate in your opinion.

    a. _____

       _____

    b. _____

       _____

    c. _____

       _____

3. Now discuss your opinions in small groups or with the entire class. Then, make a group decision.

Thinking About Reading for a Purpose

In this unit, you began by being given a task to do. In order to do the Unit Task, it was necessary to find information in the seven readings in the unit. Think about how you did this, and answer these questions:

1. What did you do before you began to read each text?

2. Did you read all of the texts in the same way? If you read some differently, what were some of these different ways (for example, skimming, scanning, reading closely)?

3. What did you do after you read each text?

4. How many times did you read each text? Why? Do you think this is common in academic reading?

5. Were all of the readings equally useful for the Unit Task? Did any of the readings give more information than others? Why or why not?

6. Now, can you explain how to read for a purpose in your own words, based upon your experience in this unit?

PART C EXPANSION ACTIVITIES

Applying Your Knowledge

1. Write and perform a role play about the life situations presented in this unit. Divide the roles among the members of the class. You can role play people you don't know much about, if you wish (such as Robert Crowley's ex-wife, Lydia Montgomery's old boyfriend, or Karen Wang's husband). The student who plays the role of the judge should ask the other students questions. The candidates for custody of the children can add information, but it must fit with the information already in the readings. For example, Robert Crowley cannot say that he is not divorced.

2. Write the transcript for another member of the family testifying before the judge.

3. Ask some parents you know what arrangements they have made for their children if they, the parents, should die. You may ask classmates, teachers, or other students. How did the parents make this decision? Are they happy with their choice?

4. Talk to a social worker about any experiences that he or she might have had with this type of case.

The Electronic Link

Information on Legal Guardians

Look on the Internet to find more information about legal guardians. One possible Internet site is:

http://www.cyberstation.net/~paralegal/guardian.htm

You can find more Internet sites devoted to family issues by using these key words to search:

adoption   guardianship

family issues   legal guardians

guardian

For More Information

If you want to know more about choosing guardians, you can contact:

Consumer Information Center
P.O. Box 100
Pueblo, CO 81002
U.S.A.

See the Additional Readings for this unit on pages 204–205.

Essay Questions

Choose one of the topics below and write an essay about it.

1. Some people believe that it is always better to leave children with family members if the children's parents should die. Do you agree? Why or why not?

2. Imagine that you are the judge. Write your opinion about this case. Be sure to give reasons for your decision.

3. Compare the law in the United States regarding guardianship of minor children with your country's laws. What would happen in your country in a case such as this?

Evaluating Your Progress

Think about the strategies that you used in this unit. Check (✓) the correct boxes.

	NEVER	SOMETIMES	OFTEN	ALWAYS
1. I was able to predict correctly the information that I would find in a reading.	☐	☐	☐	☐
2. When I previewed, I thought about where a reading came from and what I knew about the topic.	☐	☐	☐	☐
3. I was able to predict the purpose of a reading.	☐	☐	☐	☐
4. I was able to recognize titles and names.	☐	☐	☐	☐
5. I was able to find the topics of paragraphs.	☐	☐	☐	☐
6. I was able to ignore technical vocabulary when necessary.	☐	☐	☐	☐
7. I was able to make inferences as I read.	☐	☐	☐	☐
8. I looked for language signals as I read.	☐	☐	☐	☐
9. I was able to guess the meaning of unknown words by using affixes.	☐	☐	☐	☐
10. I thought about parts of speech when I was trying to figure out the meaning of unknown words.	☐	☐	☐	☐

Setting Your Reading Goals

Choose three items from the list above that you would like to improve. Write them on the lines below.

Goal #1: _____

Goal #2: _____

Goal #3: _____

IN THIS UNIT

Reading Strategies

- Examining organization: process
- Understanding and using subtitles
- Understanding how information is organized
- Understanding the format of a text
- Understanding what words refer to: personal pronouns
- Understanding what words refer to: *this* and *that*
- Summarizing

- Examining organization
- Understanding the author's tone
- Understanding the use of examples
- Looking for guiding sentences

Strategies for Unknown Vocabulary

- Using synonyms to guess words in context
- Using examples to guess words in context
- Understanding the general meaning of unknown words

The Art and Science of Movie Making

Think About It

Look at the pictures on page 46. What kind of movie is each one from? Do you like to go to the movies? What kinds of movies do you usually see?

Looking Ahead in Unit Two

Look at each of the readings in the unit. Match the readings in the unit with the types of readings listed below. Write the reading numbers on the lines. How do you know which kind of reading each one is? (Some types of readings appear more than once in this unit.)

	READING NUMBER(S)
1. an encyclopedia article	_____
2. a newspaper article	_____
3. a chapter from a book	_____
4. a magazine article	_____

Looking at the Unit Tasks

This unit has two tasks. The first one occurs after Reading 3 on page 68. You will do the second one after Reading 6 on page 93. Look for the two Unit Tasks and write their titles below.

Unit Task 1   _____

Unit Task 2   _____

Identify the Information You Need

1. **Read the instructions for Unit Task 1 on page 68. Think about the information that you will need to do it. Write questions that will help you to do Unit Task 1 on the lines below.**

   1. _____?

   2. _____?

   3. _____?

   4. _____?

   5. _____?

2. **Compare your questions with your classmates' questions. Are there any questions that you want to add to your list? Copy your final list of questions into your notebook.**

3. **Now look ahead to Readings 1–3. Which of them might give you the answers to each of the questions in your notebook? Write the question numbers and the reading numbers on the lines below.**

QUESTION NUMBER	READING NUMBER(S)
_____	_____
_____	_____
_____	_____
_____	_____
_____	_____

READING 1: "MOTION PICTURES"

Step 1: Preview the Reading

1. **Where is this text from? Do you expect it to contain facts or opinions? Why?**

PREVIEWING STRATEGY: Using Background Knowledge

Before you begin to read a text, it is often useful to think of what you already know about the topic or the subject of the reading. You may not think that you know very much about a topic, but even general information that you know can help you to understand the reading more easily.

---

2. **What do you know about how movies are made? Discuss your ideas with your classmates. These questions may help you.**

  1. Who are some famous movie-makers?

  2. What are their jobs?

  3. What place is famous for making movies?

  4. How long does it take to make a movie?

  5. How much does it cost to make a movie?

  6. What kinds of things have to be done in order to make a movie?

3. **Read the title of the following reading. Would you expect some parts of this article to be in chronological order? Why or why not? Quickly read the first sentence of each paragraph. Are some parts in chronological order? Give examples to support your answer.**

4. **Look back at the list of questions you wrote in your notebook for Unit Task 1. Which questions do you think this article may answer? Put a check mark (✓) next to them.**

Step 2: Read Closely

1. **Read the text. The first time you read, cover up the margin questions. Look for the answers to the questions you checked in your notebook. Write any answers that you find next to your questions.**

2. **Read the text again. Use the margin questions to help you.**

READING 1

Motion Pictures
From *Book of Knowledge,* 1989

1   The key people in movie productions are the producer and the director. The producer usually chooses the story or the idea behind the movie, borrows the money to make the movie and decides on the director and the principal actors. In general, the producer begins the process of movie making by choosing a script or an idea for a movie. The director controls the filming of the picture and is the mastermind behind the finished movie. Occasionally, pictures are produced and directed by the same person.

2   Before the movie production can be started, the script must be prepared. In the early days of movie making, stories were usually written especially for the movies. Today, they are often taken from successful plays or novels.

3   Whether the producer chooses to take a story from a play or novel or use a new story, a screenplay needs to be written. When a play or novel is used, writers adapt or rewrite the story to make it more suitable for a movie. First, they arrange the story into scenes. They may add new scenes or characters. Then writers either adapt dialogue from the original work or completely rewrite it.

4   After the screenplay is written, the technical crew is put together. The art director, the costume designer, the

1. What is the main idea of this paragraph?

2. What is the purpose of paragraphs 2 and 3?

3. Does paragraph 5 explain one of the steps in making a film?

4. What is the relationship in paragraph 6 between the words *design* and *designer*?

5. In paragraph 7, how does the writer explain what a *montage expert* is?

6. What is the relationship in paragraph 8 between *director* and *direction* ?

7. What part of the film making process is described in paragraphs 9 and 10?

8. What part of making a film is explained in paragraph 11?

makeup people, the camera operator and many other specialists are all part of the technical and stage crews.

5   The art director has a very important job. He or she oversees the general appearance of the locations or sets, the costumes and the actors. Movies are photographed on specially built sets or on location. Movies shot "on location" are filmed in natural settings. That is, a movie that takes place in a well-known city such as New York is usually filmed in that city's actual streets and buildings. If part of the movie is set in the mountains or by the sea, the art director will look for a real place that fits the script. The art director must also plan for special effects. Perhaps the movie includes a landslide. Of course, it would be impossible to create a real landslide. Instead, the art director arranges to have a false landslide take place on a small copy of a mountain. The art director also designs buildings or sometimes whole towns as sets for the scenes that are not shot on location. For some movies, the art director must copy the exact style of buildings at the time.

6   The costume designer works with the art director and matches the style of the clothes with the time of the story. The makeup specialists not only use regular makeup to make the actors appear more attractive, but many times they must also use special makeup to transform the appearance of the actors. For example, sometimes an actor needs to play a character who is much older. It is the job of the makeup people to make the actor appear the right age.

7   Another technical specialist is the montage expert. A montage is used to show the quick passage of time in the story. For instance, six months of a singer's career can be shown in six minutes by a montage expert. The expert could show a quick sequence of shots of a concert hall, an airplane taking off, a Christmas tree, another concert hall and finally a spring

thunderstorm. If the montage is well done, the audience believes that time has passed.

8   The director and the experts give their ideas to the camera operator. Although there is a general camera plan for each scene, the director often changes his mind during the filming. The chief camera operator is responsible for following the director's orders but rarely actually touches a camera. The filming is actually done by a group of assistants working under the chief camera operator's direction.

Filming the Movie

9   When a film is ready to be photographed, it is not shot in chronological order. The script is divided into numbered scenes. All the scenes that will be shot on the same sets or in the same location are shot at the same time. Usually outdoor or location scenes are shot first. Then the indoor scenes are shot in a regular film studio.

10   Often a scene is practiced before it is shot. Even after the scene has been worked out, if the director thinks that the scene is not going well, he stops the filming by shouting "Cut!" Sometimes the director is satisfied with the first shot or "take." But more often, dozens of takes are made of the same scene. At the end of the day, the director goes over the rushes. Rushes are prints of scenes filmed that day. If the director does not like the rushes, the scenes are refilmed.

11   It may take from 20 days to several months to finish a picture. When all the photography is finished, the prints of the film go to the film editor or cutter. The editor takes the separate shots and puts them together in a pattern. Most directors also supervise the editing or cutting of their pictures. The film is then put together in what is called a rough cut. The recorded music is placed on the sound track along with the dialogue. The editor and the director then look at the rough cut and make the final arrangement of shots.

A. Checking Your Comprehension

1. Complete the chart below with information from Reading 1.

Job title	What he/she does
producer	
director	
	writes the screenplay
art director	
	designs the clothes
make-up specialist	
	chooses scenes to show that time has passed
chief camera operator	
	actually films the movie
editor	

2. Number the steps in the process of movie making. The first one has been done for you.

____ a. The location shots are filmed.

____ b. The screenplay is written.

____ c. The director is chosen.

____ d. The technical crew is assembled.

__1__ e. The producer chooses an idea and borrows money.

____ f. The rough cut is made.

____ g. The actors are chosen.

____ h. The film is edited.

3. What two things about film making does this reading explain?

B. Making Inferences

What inferences can you make about the reading? Answer the questions below.

1. Does it take much money to make a movie? Support your answer with information from the reading.

2. Is it important for movies to look realistic? Support your answer with information from the reading.

3. What do you think might be some of the problems a producer might have when trying to make a movie?

C. Topics for Discussion

Discuss the following questions with your classmates.

1. Which of the jobs in Reading 1 is the most important? Why?

2. Would you like to make movies? Why or why not? If you would, which job would you prefer?

3. Have you ever tried filming someone or something with a video camera? Was it easy? What would have made your results better?

D. Reading Strategies

READING STRATEGY: Examining Organization: Process

Some parts of Reading 1 of Unit 1 were organized chronologically. It used dates and times in order to establish the order of events.

The text that you just read (Reading 1 of Unit 2) also uses chronological order part of the time. Does it use dates and times to make that order clear? If not, what kinds of words does it use to show the reader the order of events?

---

1. **Look back at the reading. Underline all of the sentences that show the order of events in the process of making a movie. Which words do you notice most often? Write the words and the paragraph you found them in below. An example has been done for you.**

   1. _before (paragraph 2)_   3. _____

   2. _____   4. _____

READING STRATEGY:
More Practice Finding Paragraph Topics

As you learned in Unit 1, all of the ideas in a paragraph should be related to the same topic. Understanding the topic of a paragraph is closely related to understanding the main ideas of a text because most of the text's important ideas will be related to the topics of different paragraphs.

---

2. **Look at these paragraphs. Do they describe the steps for making a movie in order? If not, what is the topic of each one of them?**

PARAGRAPH #	TOPIC
5	
6	
7	
8	

E. Strategies for Unknown Vocabulary

VOCABULARY STRATEGY:
Using Synonyms to Guess Words in Context

Sometimes a writer defines a technical word by giving another word with a similar meaning (a synonym). Synonyms are often introduced with the word **or.** In these cases, **or** is a signal that the author is explaining the meaning.

Look at these sentences. In which one does **or** introduce a synonym?

Producers often choose to use a story from **a play or a novel**.

Sometimes the director is satisfied with the **first shot, or "take."**

What is that synonym?

---

1. **Read the sentences below. In which sentences does *or* introduce a synonym? Check (✓) your answers.**

   _✓_ 1. When all the photography is finished, the prints of the film go to the film editor, or cutter.

   ____ 2. Then writers either adapt dialogue from the original work or completely rewrite it.

   ____ 3. She oversees the general appearance of the locations, or sets.

   ____ 4. Today, they are often taken from successful plays or novels.

   ____ 5. The producer usually chooses the story or the idea behind the movie.

   ____ 6. They may add new scenes or characters.

   _✓_ 7. The appearance of the actors can be transformed, or changed, by make-up.

When a word is difficult to define or does not have a synonym, a writer may help readers by giving them an example. Examples are often introduced by phrases such as:

for example   for instance   that is

What term in the reading does this example from paragraph 5 explain?

That is, a movie that takes place in a well-known city, such as New York, is usually filmed in that city's actual streets and buildings.

2. **Find the examples that help to explain these words. Write them on the lines.**

1. special effects   (paragraph 5) *special built sets or on location*

2. transform   (paragraph 6) _____

3. montage   (paragraph 7) _____

Step 3: Note Useful Information

1. **Reading 1 describes the process of how a movie is made and the different responsibilities of people who work on a movie. Which of these two kinds of information will probably be more useful for Unit Task 1? Why?**

2. **Go back to Reading 1 and highlight or underline those sections that you think will be useful for Unit Task 1.**

F. Building Your Vocabulary

One way to learn new words is to make a word web. Look at the word web on the next page for the different jobs involved in movie making.

1. Why is the word *producer* in the center? Find the words *writers,* and *screenplay.* What arc thcy attachcd to? Why?

2. Now use the words in the box to fill the correct circles in the web.

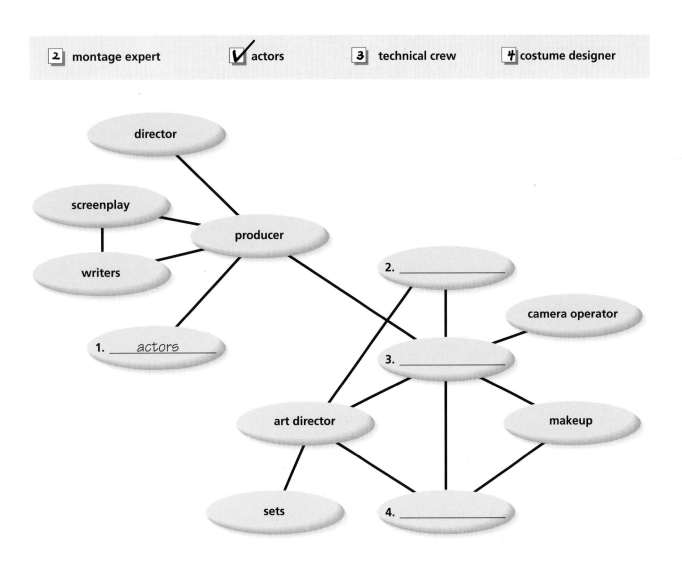

3. Add any other words to the web which were new to you in Reading 1.

4. Now look at the word web and cross out any words that you do not think will be useful for Unit Task 1.

5. Look at the words below. Circle the words that you think will be useful for Unit Task 1. Add them to the word web above.

special effects	scene	montage	shot	sequence
audience	take	rushes	character	cutting
dialogue	rough cut	sound track		

6. Compare your word web with your classmates' word webs. What words did they add? Where did they put them?

G. Writing Your Ideas

Look at the writing topics below. Choose at least one and write about it.

1. Take an interesting story that you know and try rewriting part of it into a screenplay. What are some of the things you need to do first? (Hint: Look at the part of Reading 1 that explains about writing a screenplay. You may also want to look at Additional Reading 3 on pages 208–211.) You may do this alone, with a partner, or with a group of classmates.

2. Compare a movie you have seen and the book that it was based on. Are they the same? If not, how was the movie different from the book? Why do you think changes were made?

3. In your own words, write the story line of a movie you have seen. Explain what happens and what each character does in the movie.

READING 2: "HOW TO TELL STORIES IN VIDEO"

Step 1: Preview the Reading

1. **Look at the title of this reading. Who is the expected audience?**

2. **How is the author's purpose similar to or different from the author's purpose in Reading 1?**

3. **Think about your general knowledge on this subject. What ideas or words in Reading 1 will probably relate to this reading?**

4. **Think about Unit Task 1. Is your purpose in reading this text the same as the purpose of the writer's intended audience? Why or why not? Will this reading be useful? How?**

5. **Look back at the list of questions you wrote in your notebook for Unit Task 1. Which questions do you think this reading may answer? Put a check mark (✓) next to them. Can you think of any other useful questions that this reading may answer?**

Step 2: Read Closely

1. **Read the text. The first time you read, cover up the margin questions. Look for the answers to the questions you checked in your notebook. Write any answers that you find next to your questions.**

2. **Read the text again. Use the margin questions to help you.**

How to Tell Stories in Video

by James Schmidt

Introduction

1   Telling stories in video is more complicated than telling them in words. When you write a story, you can give the reader a lot of background information about the characters and the location. When people watch a video, they can get some of this information from dialogue, but much of it comes from the types of shots that you choose to include.

2   Different types of shots can give very different messages. For example, a character can appear powerful or weak, depending on the type of shot you use. Similarly, one type of shot might make a situation seem dangerous and another might make the same situation funny.

1. _____ CU

2. reverse-angle shot

1. How has the author made the technical vocabulary clearer for his readers?

3   The following are some of the basic shots:
- an establishing shot
- a medium shot
- a close-up

An *establishing shot* (ES) shows the location, introduces the characters and explains the relationship between the characters and the location. /3

A *medium shot* (MS) moves the action forward. It gives us the next piece of information we need to understand. 5

A *close-up* (CU) gives more intimate information about a character's emotions and personality. 4

3. _____ ES

2. If you do not understand the word *angle*, continue reading and look for more information to help you.

4   There are several other types of shots including reverse angle, point-of-view, reaction shot, extreme close-up and extreme wide-angle.

A *reverse angle* (RA) is a shot taken from the opposite angle of the previous shot. For example, the first shot might show a group of people watching something. The reverse angle shot would then show what they are watching.

A *point-of-view* (POV) shot is taken from a character's point of view: the camera, and therefore the audience, sees what the character sees. This type of shot helps the audience understand the character better and usually 1

4. _____ POV

5. _____ MS RS

makes them feel more sympathetic to this character.

A *reaction shot* (RS) is a medium or close-up view of the character reacting to what she or he has just seen, felt, or heard.

5   A <u>good</u> director varies the shots. For example, he or she moves from a wide shot to a medium shot, then to a close-up and back to another medium shot. This technique gives variety to the story and helps to tell it in an interesting way. You should choose the shots in your video to advance the story and hold interest.

6.

7.

8. <u>low-angle shot</u>

6   You can change the mood of a scene with the angles that you choose. Directors use this tool to help them tell their story. Angle changes can make a scene seem more dramatic, add a new idea or provide a fresh viewpoint. Here are a few common angles you should know:

High-angle shot. This means shooting the character from above. This makes the character appear smaller or dependent.

Low-angle shot. This means shooting the character from below. This makes the character appear larger and more powerful.

Eye-level shot. This means shooting at eye level. This type of angle makes the character appear to be an equal—neither dependent nor in control. For this reason, it is usually better to shoot people at eye level, unless you want to make them seen more powerful or more dependent.

7   Another problem that you will have to solve is that people do not usually stay in one place for very long. For example, a character may begin speaking while they are standing, then walk across a room and sit down. As the director, your job is to figure out where to put the camera. Often you have to compromise, or find a middle ground. One compromise would be to put the camera halfway between a sitting and standing height. However, this might not be the best solution. One common answer is to keep the camera at a standing-position height. This solution works because it is normal to look down at someone who is seated as you talk to them.

3. What is the main idea of this paragraph?

4. How does the author try to help you to understand the word *compromise?*

A. Checking Your Comprehension

1. **Label photos 1–5 on page 57 with the names of different shots (establishing shot, close-up, point-of-view, reaction shot, ~~reverse angle shot~~). An example has been done for you.**

2. **Label photos 6–8 on page 58 with the names of different angles (high angle, ~~low angle,~~ eye level). An example has been done for you.**

B. Making Inferences

Guess which types of shots and/or angles a director might choose in each situation. Give reasons for your answers.

1. a young woman who is very upset because her mother has just died

2. a small child who is lost in a crowd of people

3. a car chase

4. a young man who beats up the neighborhood bully

5. the opening shot in a movie

C. Topics for Discussion

Discuss the following questions with your classmates.

1. How can different camera angles give impressions that are not true or real? Can you think of some other ways in which shots in a film can fool the audience?

2. Have you ever seen an IMAX movie or a film taken with several cameras? What is the effect of this? Do you like it? Why or why not?

D. Reading Strategies

READING STRATEGY: Understanding and Using Subtitles

Reading 2 is an example of a nonfiction text. We use the word *nonfiction* to describe texts which are not just stories, but describe some part of real life. Writers of nonfiction often use subtitles to help guide the reader. The subtitles usually give the general topic of the main sections of the reading.

There is one subtitle in this reading. What is it?

If you were going to add two other subtitles, which of these would you choose? Why?

Changing Angles	Using Point-of-View Shots
The Uses of Close-ups	Types of Shots

Where would you put them?

---

1. **Look back at Reading 2 and write the two new subtitles on the lines provided on pages 57 and 58.**

READING STRATEGY:
Understanding How Information is Organized

We saw that Reading 1 was loosely organized according to the steps in the process of making a movie, along with many descriptions of different jobs. Although Reading 2 explains how to do something, is it organized as steps in a process? If not, how is it organized? Which clues help you to understand this?

The best way to describe the organization of Reading 2 is as a *list*. It is a list of definitions and explanations of different kinds of movie shots. However, within this list, the author additionally organized the information in a certain way.

2. **Look back at Reading 2. Can you see why the author put the different shots in the order that he did? Does this order make the information easier to understand? Why or why not?**

READING STRATEGY: Understanding the Format of a Text

Writers often use different types of printing and other formatting features to help readers understand their message. Some of the most common formatting features are:

putting words in bold type

putting words in italics

<u>underlining</u>

making some words larger

What is the effect of changing the format like this?

Writers generally try to make sure that each feature has the same purpose every time it is used. For example, in this textbook a larger size and a different color of type is used for the names of the different sections of each unit, such as Checking Your Comprehension, Reading Strategies, etc.

How do these formatting features help you to use this textbook?

3. **Look back at Reading 2. Complete the table below with the formatting features in the reading and explain what each one is used for.**

Type of feature	What it is used for

Step 3: Note Useful Information

1. **Look back at Reading 2. One section is probably less useful for Unit Task 1 than the other two sections. Which one is it? Why?**

2. **Look back at the two important sections and underline or highlight the most important information in them. Use the formatting features to help you to decide which information is important.**

E. Building Your Vocabulary

Use these steps to build your vocabulary with words from the reading.

1. Look back at Reading 2. Choose words to add to your vocabulary notebook. There is a lot of technical vocabulary in this unit. Some of it will be necessary for the Unit Task, and some will not be. Choose the words that you think will be most useful in discussing the Unit Task. You should also choose words that you think will be generally useful.

2. Copy a sentence or phrase where you found each word and write the meaning in your own words, including the part of speech. If you are still unsure of the meaning, look it up in a dictionary and write the meaning in your own words in your vocabulary notebook.

3. Check (✓) the words in your list that you think will be important for the Unit Task.

F. Writing Your Ideas

Look at the writing topics below. Choose at least one and write about it.

1. Watch several commercials on television. Try to notice how different camera shots are used to give different impressions of people and products. Write about what you discover.

2. Watch a movie and look for some of the different camera angles that are used. Describe the effect that they have and explain whether you think they did a good job or not.

Step 1: Preview the Reading

PREVIEWING STRATEGY: Skimming

When we skim a reading, we read through it very quickly to get a general idea of its content. When we skim, we do not read every word; we do not even read every line. Our eyes pass over the text slowly enough to understand some words or phrases but not slowly enough to understand all of the ideas. When we skim, we often look for titles, subtitles, and other specially formatted words or expressions. We also try to notice the general organization of the reading.

The techniques of scanning and skimming are related, but their purposes are different. When we scan, we are looking for specific information such as dates, names, or certain words or phrases. (For more information on scanning, see page xvi.)

---

1. **Skim Reading 3. What do you think the author's purpose is? Is the author's purpose probably more similar to the purpose in Reading 1 or Reading 2?**

2. **Now scan the reading to find the name(s) of movies. What formatting feature helps you to find these easily?**

3. **Scan the reading to find out what kinds of special effects are discussed. What formatting feature helps you to find this information easily?**

4. **What do you know about "special effects"? What can you remember from Reading 1? Have you seen either of the movies mentioned in the text or any other movie with a lot of special effects? Tell the class about it.**

5. **Look back at the list of questions you wrote in your notebook for Unit Task 1. Which questions do you think this reading may answer? Put a check mark (✓) next to them. Can you think of any other useful questions that this reading may answer?**

Step 2: Read Closely

1. **Read the text. The first time you read, cover up the margin questions. Look for the answers to the questions you checked in your notebook. Write any answers that you find next to your questions.**

2. **Read the text again. Use the margin questions to help you.**

CHAPTER 2: THE MAGIC OF SPECIAL EFFECTS

MOTION CONTROL AT WORK

1 There are many different kinds of special effects. One of the most common special effects puts together images from two separate pieces of film. In the past, in order to do this, it was necessary to photograph each part with a camera fixed in one position. A new camera system called the Motion Control Camera made it possible to move the camera. This freedom of movement makes the shot look much more realistic.

1. What is the purpose of this paragraph?

2 For example, imagine that a director wanted to show some people running away from a large ball of fire. Before the invention of the Motion Control System he or she had to black out the area above the people—the area where the ball of fire would appear—when the people were filmed. Then the ball of fire was filmed by itself. When both images were put together, the ball of fire filled in the blacked-out area above the people and the special effect was completed.

2. How are paragraphs 3 and 4 related?

3 The new Motion Control System's computer memory has changed all of this. This new system allows the camera operators to move the camera across the scene. This makes it seem more realistic. They film the actors with the area blacked out above them as before but move the camera at the speed and angle they desire. The computer in the system remembers the exact speed and angle and will copy the camera movement exactly when they film the ball of fire.

4 Of course, the computer can copy the same speed and angle of camera movement again and again. That means it is possible to put together as many different elements as a director wants in order to make the final image. This is how hundreds of spaceships can be seen fighting and interacting in a film such as *Star Wars.*

MODELS

5 Of all of the fantastic effects that we have seen in the *Star Wars* series, perhaps the most important one is the very first one the audience saw at the opening of the first film. If that one had not worked so well, if it had not gotten the audience's attention and made them believe that they were watching real spaceships in action, the movie wouldn't have been nearly as successful.

3. What helps you to guess the meaning of *model?*

6 That shot was made using a model that was just over three feet long. Models were used in many places on *Star Wars.* They were just as important to its spectacular special effects as the Motion Control Camera. Models vary in size depending on the kind of shot that is needed. In the movie, *The Empire Strikes Back,* they varied in size from two inches tall for distance shots, to up to four feet tall for close-ups.

4. Does this paragraph give you enough information to guess the meaning of *depth?*

7   Some shots require models that add depth to a particular scene. In order to do this, special effects experts make a model which is very wide in the front and narrow at the back. When the model is filmed from the front, it looks much longer than it is. When it is seen on the screen, viewers think they are seeing a spacecraft which looks several miles long.

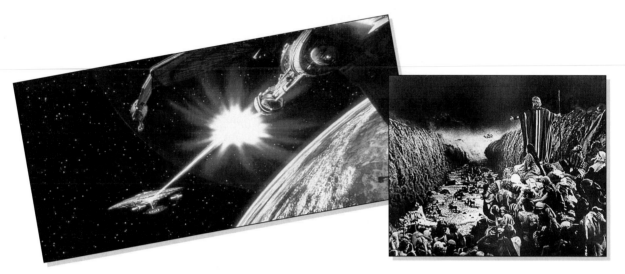

MATTE ART

5. If you do not understand the phrase *matte artist,* keep reading and looking for information to help you.

8   Another important technique in creating special effects like the ones used in *Star Wars* is done by the matte artist. A film such as *Star Wars* would have been too expensive to make if all of the film's sets had had to be completely built. To keep costs down and at the same time create realistic settings, the film producer used a matte artist to produce painted settings. Sometimes matte artists also rescue film that has already been shot but contains a mistake. A historical movie, for example, might require outside locations. Sometimes, nearby modern buildings mistakenly appear in a scene when it is filmed. The matte artist is then called in to paint over the unnecessary buildings.

6. Does the author explain the meaning of *matte shot?*

9   A matte shot is a combination of live action and painting which has been very carefully made to match the live action in every detail. There are two common methods for creating matte shots. Often a painting is made ahead of time and filmed when the live action itself is filmed. This is done by making the painting on glass which is put in front of the camera. Sometimes the painting is made after the live action has been filmed. To do this, the artist projects the film onto glass, paints in the new detail, and then re-photographs the glass painting and the filmed scene together. This creates a new image.

10 For example, in one *Star Wars* scene a character walks across a narrow ledge next to an incredibly high cliff. In reality, the ledge was only three feet above the floor. The depth was created by the matte artist.

A. Checking Your Comprehension

Complete the outline with three kinds of special effects techniques that are mentioned in the reading.

1. Technique   <u>Motion Control Camera</u>

    a. Uses   _____

                _____

    b. Advantages   _____

                _____

2. Technique   _____

    a. Uses   _____

                _____

    b. Advantages   <u>saves production time and money</u>

                _____

3. Technique   _____

    a. Uses   _____

                _____

    b. Advantages   <u>fixes mistakes</u>

                _____

B. Making Inferences

Which of these statements do you think we can infer, based on the information in Reading 3? Circle them.

1. The author admires the special effects work in *Star Wars*.

2. The author has probably mentioned *Star Wars* earlier in the book.

3. Films that are more realistic are considered better.

4. The opening scene of *Star Wars* was not very effective.

5. Special effects can help decrease the cost of a film and make it possible to show dangerous-looking scenes without putting actors in real danger.

C. Topics for Discussion

Discuss the following questions with your classmates.

1. Do you like films that have a lot of special effects? Why or why not?

2. Have you seen *King Kong* or *Godzilla?* Can you think of some scenes where special effects were used? What do you think of the special effects in those movies?

D. Reading Strategies

READING STRATEGY:
Understanding What Words Refer to: Personal Pronouns

Writers often use personal pronouns (**he, she, they, it**) rather than repeat the same words again and again. You are probably very familiar with some of these pronouns. When you read, it is very important to understand what each of these pronouns refers to.

For example, in the paragraph below,

we	refers to the reader and the author
it	refers to the special effect in the opening scene
them and **they**	refer to the audience

Of all of the fantastic effects that **we** have seen in the *Star Wars* series, perhaps the most important one is the very first one the audience saw at the opening of the first film. If that one had not worked so well, if **it** had not gotten the audience's attention and made **them** believe that **they** were watching real spaceships in action, the movie wouldn't have been nearly as successful.

What does each of these personal pronouns refer to in the following paragraph?

Some shots require models to be made so that **they** add depth to a particular scene. In order to do this, special effects experts make a model which is very wide in the front and narrow at the back. When the model is filmed from the front, **it** looks much longer than **it** is. When **it** is seen on the screen, viewers think **they** are seeing a spacecraft which looks several miles long.

---

1. **Circle the personal pronouns in this paragraph and explain what they refer to.**

The new Motion Control System's computer memory has changed all of this. This new system allows the camera operators to move the camera across the scene. This makes it seem more realistic. They film the actors with the area blacked out above them as before, but move the camera at the speed and angle they desire. The computer in the system remembers the exact speed and angle and will copy the camera movement exactly when they film the ball of fire.

In addtion to personal pronouns, there are other words we can use to refer to nouns and noun phrases. In this text, **this** and **that** are two of those words. They may occur before a noun (for example, **this book, that boy**) or stand alone (for example, **This is mine. That is hers.**).

What do the words in bold refer to in the following sentence?

One of the most common special effects puts together images from two separate pieces of film. In the past, in order to do **this**, it was necessary to photograph each part with a camera fixed in one position. A new camera system called the Motion Control Camera made it possible to move the camera. **This freedom of movement** makes the shot look much more realistic.

2. **Circle the words *this* and *that* in the paragraph below and say what they refer to.**

   1. Of course, the computer can copy the same speed and angle of camera movement again and again. That means it is possible to put together as many different elements as a director wants in order to make the final image. This is how hundreds of spaceships can be seen fighting and interacting in a film such as *Star Wars*.

   2. There are two common methods for creating matte shots. Often a painting is made ahead of time and filmed when the live action itself is filmed. This is done by making the painting on glass which is put in front of the camera. Sometimes the painting is made after the live action has been filmed. To do this, the artist projects the film onto glass, paints in the new detail and then re-photographs the glass painting and the filmed scene together. This creates a new image.

Step 3: Note Important Information

Reading 3 has a lot of technical information. Some of it is probably not necessary to do the Unit Task.

1. **Look at this list and check (✓) the ideas that you think will be important for Unit Task 1. Can you explain your choices?**

   _____ 1. why the Motion Control System is better

   _____ 2. when the Motion Control Camera is used

   _____ 3. how the Motion Control System works

   _____ 4. when models are used

   _____ 5. the size of models

   _____ 6. the job of the matte artist

   _____ 7. the two different techniques of creating a matte shot

2. **Compare your answers above with those of other classmates. Then go back to the reading and underline or highlight the important sections.**

E. Building Your Vocabulary

Use these steps to build your vocabulary with words from the reading.

1. Look back at Reading 3. Pay careful attention to the sections that you highlighted or underlined. Choose the words that you think will be most useful in discussing the Unit Task. You should also choose words that you think will be generally useful.

2. Copy the sentence or phrase where you found each word and write the definition in your own words, including the part of speech. If you are still not sure of the meaning, look the word up in your dictionary and write the meaning in your own words in your vocabulary notebook.

F. Writing Your Ideas

Look at the writing topics below. Choose at least one and write about it.

1. Do you enjoy films that have a lot of special effects? Explain the reasons for your opinion.

2. What movie or movies have special effects that you thought were very good? What did you like about them? How did they make you feel?

UNIT TASK 1:
Film Analysis

In this Unit Task, you will prepare a written or oral report on a part of a movie or television show. Your report will focus on:

- a description of how the director used different camera shots to tell the story

- a description of any special effects that were used, including your best guess on how they were done. (Remember that the work of a montage expert or a make-up person is part of special effects.)

You may do this Unit Task in a group or on your own. If you work in a group, everyone must watch the same movie or television show. It will be easier to do the Unit Task if you can make or rent a videotape of the movie or television show that you want to analyze. Depending on the film, eight to ten minutes is probably a long enough section to analyze. Do not try to analyze too large a section of the movie or television show. Choose a continuous section that has several different elements that you can discuss. You could also pick out several elements from different places in the movie or television program.

Complete the following steps to help you do Unit Task 1.

1. You may want to look for a film by one of these famous directors: (Remember, it is not necessary to understand the language in order to analyze the film. A film in any language would work well for this Unit Task.)

Akira Kurosawa	François Truffaut	Charlie Chaplin	Lina Wertmüller
Alfred Hitchcock	Ingmar Bergman	Federico Fellini	Sergei Eisenstein

2. Watch the segment of the movie or television program that you are going to analyze. As you watch, complete these charts. You will probably need to watch the video several times.

Description of the scene(s): _____

_____

Characters in the scene(s): _____

_____

Relationship between the characters: _____

_____

Type of shot	Description of shot	Purpose

Description of special effects	How they might have been done

UNIT TASK 2: REVIEWING A MOVIE

For your second Unit Task you will prepare a written or oral review of a movie that you have seen.

Identify the Information You Need

1. **Read the instructions for Unit Task 2 on page 93. Think about the information that you will need to do it. Some of the information can only come from the movie that you will review. However, information about how a movie review is written and what makes a good movie can be found in the readings. Write questions that will help you to do Unit Task 2 on the lines below.**

QUESTIONS ABOUT MOVIE REVIEWS IN GENERAL:

1. _____?

2. _____?

3. _____?

QUESTIONS ABOUT HOW TO JUDGE MOVIES:

4. _____?

5. _____?

6. _____?

7. _____?

2. **Compare your questions with your classmates' questions. Are there any questions that you want to add to your list? Copy your final list of questions into your notebook.**

3. **Now look ahead to Readings 4–6. Which of them might give you the answers to each question? Write the question numbers and the reading numbers on the lines below.**

QUESTION NUMBER	READING NUMBER(S)
____	_____
____	_____
____	_____
____	_____
____	_____
____	_____
____	_____

Step 1: Preview the Reading

1. **What was the author's purpose in writing this text? In order to answer this question, where could you look?**

2. **Have you ever read a text like this?**

3. **What kinds of information do you expect to find in Reading 4? Check (✓) the boxes.**

Type of information	Must have	May have	Probably will not have
the writer's opinion about the movie			
information about the director's life and background			
some information about the story			
the names of the movie stars			
comparisons with other movies			
the names of the director and the producer			
biographical information about the stars			

4. **Do you think that this reading will help you to do Unit Task 2? Why or why not? Look back at the list of questions you wrote in your notebook for Unit Task 2. Which questions do you think this reading may answer? Put a check mark (✓) next to them.**

1. **Read the text. The first time you read, cover up the margin questions. Look for the answers to the questions you checked in your notebook. Write any answers that you find next to your questions.**

2. **Read the text again. Use the margin questions to help you.**

READING 4

This *Titanic* Floats!

by Kathryn Johnson

Producers: James Cameron, Jon Landau
Director: James Cameron
Starring: Leonardo DiCaprio, Kate Winslet, Billy Zane, Kathy Bates
Rated: PG-13, violence, nudity, some strong language
Running time: 3 hours, 14 minutes

1   Those of you who have enjoyed director James Cameron's science fiction hits such as *Aliens*, *The Abyss* and *The Terminator* may be surprised at his newest movie. *Titanic* is an old-fashioned romance with incredible special effects.

2   *Titanic* is an epic that women will love to cry at, with a leading man (Leonardo DiCaprio) that they will love to look at. However, men will also have a good time at this movie. There's plenty of action, from walls of water, to collapsing staircases, to falling smokestacks. Cameron also thoughtfully provided the beautiful Kate Winslet for the men to admire. In short, no one from eight to eighty will be bored watching *Titanic* (all three-plus hours of it!)

3   The plot is tried-and-true. Kate Winslet plays Rose DeWitt Bukater. She is the only daughter of a Philadelphia society matron who has fallen on hard times. Rose and her domineering mother (Frances Fisher) are returning from vacation in Europe.

Cal Hockley (Billy Zane), Rose's fiancé is traveling with them. He is very rich, but very nasty. Only a self-centered, social-climbing mother could want this guy for a son-in-law.

4   As anyone could easily predict, Rose doesn't love Cal. Why should she? He treats her like a piece of property. She is only marrying him to please her mother. In addition, Rose feels trapped by the social rules of the upper class. At the beginning of the movie, Rose recalls her trip on the Titanic, as "…a slave ship, taking me back to America in chains."

5   Suddenly, we see Rose running across the deck to commit suicide by jumping off the ship. Cameron doesn't provide enough background for such a desperate act but he needed a way for Rose and the hero Jack Dawson (Leonardo DiCaprio) to meet. The scene is unrealistic but it gets the job done. Jack is a poor but bold artist who had already noticed Rose from afar.

6   This is where the film starts to take off. It has all of the elegance and romance of a 1940s Hollywood film. In true Hollywood fashion, Rose introduces young Jack to civilized upper-class society, horrifying her mother and making her fiancé very jealous. In return, Jack shows her that you don't have to be rich to have fun, and teaches her to spit like a man.

Margin questions:

1. So far, do you think that the writer liked the movie? Why do you think so?

2. What is the purpose of the parentheses ( )?

3. What is the purpose of paragraphs 3–6?

4. How is paragraph 8 a little different from the rest of the review?

7 The romance between Jack and Rose takes up the first half of the movie. Then the iceberg hits and we see Cameron at his best. The special effects are the most amazing that he (or any other director) has ever put on the screen. This is his true strength as a director.

8 Of course, no film is without its faults. One major problem is that not enough is done with the minor characters. For example, Danny Nucci's role as Jack's friend is left completely undeveloped. And Kathy Bates is wonderful as Molly Brown, but we don't see enough of her. In addition, the main characters are stereotypes. Rose is beautiful and sweet. Jack is poor but honest. And Cal is thoroughly evil. However, despite these faults, you will find yourself caring about and believing in these people.

9 The computer-generated special effects are simply awesome. There will be no doubt in your mind that the Titanic *is* sinking. However, other scenes, such as crowd scenes, are not as believable. Cameron uses computer images most effectively to connect the past to the present. For example, he shows us the wreck of the Titanic lying on the floor of the ocean and then magically it becomes the ship moving through the sea.

5. What is the purpose of paragraphs 10–11?

10 No one knows if *Titanic* will make money or not. With a price tag of $200 million, it will have to do very, very well both in the United States and abroad. The simple story should help. Movie-goers all over the world will be able to identify with Rose, Jack and the rest of the passengers on that unlucky ship. Whether or not the film is a financial success, Cameron has succeeded in making a wonderful romantic epic.

11 Despite some flaws, this *Titanic* really does float. Don't miss it.

FACTS ABOUT TITANIC: THE SHIP AND THE MOVIE

How long did the ship take to sink?
Under three hours.

How long is the movie?
3 hours, 14 minutes.

How much did the Titanic (the ship) cost?
About $7.5 million in 1912.

How much did Titanic (the movie) cost?
About $200 million in 1997.

How long did it take to make the movie?
160 days.

How much did the costumes cost?
$8.4 million.

The movie set:
40 acres in Rosarito Beach, Mexico.

The studio included:
A replica of the Titanic which was only 10% smaller than the original ship. It floated in a 17 million gallon outdoor tank. The deck was 45 feet above the water. Individual sets were made of the ship's dining room and staircase. These were built at the bottom of a 30 foot tank which held 5 million gallons of water. The dishes and carpeting were made by the same manufacturers who had made the originals.

The number of computer-generated shots:
550

Number of people in the technical crew:
There were 800 people in the technical crew including 80 electricians, 30 lifeguards, 100 stunt people and 50 emergency medical personnel.

1. Complete the chart with information from the reading.

1. Movie title ___Titanic___

2. Director ___James Cameron___

3. Main characters
   ___Jack Dawson___
   ___Rose DeWitt Bukater___
   ___Cal Hodzley___

4. Played by
   ___Leonardo Cameron DiCaprio___
   ___Kat Winslet___
   ___Billy Zane___

5. Minor characters
   ___Molly Brown___
   ___Phila-delphia___
   _____

6. Played by
   ___Kathy Bates___
   ___Frances Fisher___
   _____

7. Good points of the movie ___romantic___

   specific examples _____

   _____

8. Criticisms of the movie _____

   specific examples _____

   _____

9. Comparisons with other movies _____

   _____

10. Writer's overall opinion _____

B. Making Inferences

Movie reviewers do not always make direct statements such as, "I really liked this movie" or "I disliked this movie." It is often up to the reader to infer their opinions from the statements in the review.

1. **Which of these comments show that the writer liked the movie? Which of them are negative? Which are neutral? Check (✓) the correct column. An example has been done for you.**

	Positive comment	Neutral comment	Negative comment
1. Those of you who have enjoyed director James Cameron's science fiction hits such as *Aliens, The Abyss* and *The Terminator* may be surprised at his newest movie.		✓	
2. In short, no one from eight to eighty will be bored watching *Titanic* (all three-plus hours of it!).	✓		✓
3. Cameron doesn't provide enough background for such a desperate act but he needed a way for Rose and the hero Jack Dawson (Leonardo DiCaprio) to meet.	✓		✓
4. The special effects are the most amazing that he (or any other director) has ever put on the screen. This is his true strength as a director.	✓	✓	
5. And Kathy Bates is wonderful as Molly Brown, but we don't see enough of her.	✓		✓
6. The computer-generated special effects are simply awesome.	✓		✓
7. However, other scenes, such as crowd scenes, are not as believable.			✓

2. **Overall, do you think the reviewer liked or disliked the movie?**

C. Topics for Discussion

Discuss the following questions with your classmates.

1. Reread paragraph 2. What assumptions does the writer make about men and women? In your opinion, are these assumptions correct? Do all women prefer love stories to action movies? Do all men prefer action movies?

2. In a movie review, a writer must give support for his or her opinions by telling the reader why he or she has those opinions. Do you think that this writer clearly explained his opinions? Why or why not?

3. How much are you influenced by another person's opinion of a movie? Do you ever ask your friends if they liked a movie before you go to see it? Why or why not?

D. Reading Strategies

READING STRATEGY: Summarizing

A movie review almost always contains a summary of the movie. The summary gives a very brief overview of the most important points of the movie. Even if you have never written a summary, you know something about summarizing because we do it often.

For example, when someone asks you about your weekend, do you tell them everything that you did and how you felt all of the time? How would people react if you did?

Summarizing a movie plot is similar to the summarizing that we do every day. We include enough information so that the reader understands the main idea but we leave out most of the details.

A movie summary also usually does not include surprise events and it often does not give away the ending of the movie. Can you explain why a movie summary usually does not include this information?

Look back at Reading 4. In which paragraphs does the writer give most of the summary? What doesn't the summary tell the reader?

---

1. Read this summary. Is it good? Why or why not?

The Dark Alley is the latest movie from director Karen Burns. Ms. Burns is a master of thrillers, and this film is probably her best. The movie starts in a city park on a beautiful sunny afternoon. Children are playing as their mothers sit and talk. The scene is lovely and tranquil, but it is obvious that it is going to change because in the shadows we can see a strange couple. They are watching the children and whispering. The story that follows shows how every family has its dark side and that people cannot escape their past. The plot has many twists and turns, but the most surprising thing for the audience to discover is that the kindly police sergeant is actually involved in the crime.

2. **Reread the paragraphs that give you a summary of the movie *Titanic*. Then, without looking at the text, rewrite the summary in your own words in your notebook. Compare your summary with the summaries of other students in your class. How are they the same? How are they different? Which information did you include? What did you leave out?**

READING STRATEGY: More Practice Finding Paragraph Topics

As you have already learned, every well-written text has a definite organization. As a reader, you can use that organization to help you predict what is coming. One important way of recognizing the organization is to find the topics of the paragraphs.

---

3. **Make an organizational chart of Reading 4 using the model below. Write the section headings on the lines and the paragraph numbers in the boxes. The first section has been done for you. Fill in the second section and then complete the chart in your notebook, drawing your own lines and boxes. Use all of the section headings below.**

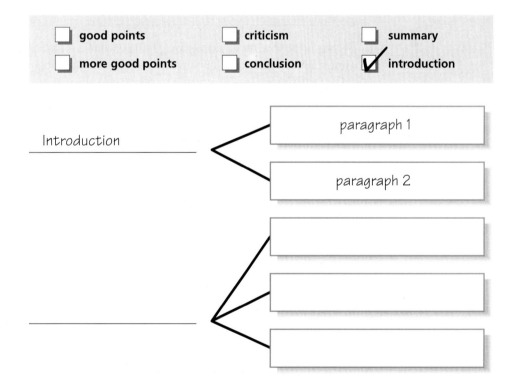

☐ good points   ☐ criticism   ☐ summary

☐ more good points   ☐ conclusion   ☑ introduction

Introduction

paragraph 1

paragraph 2

VOCABULARY STRATEGY:
Understanding the General Meaning of Unknown Words

Sometimes the reading does not give enough information to guess the exact meaning of an unknown word, but there are enough clues to guess its general meaning.

Look at this example:

He is very rich, but very nasty.

You might not be able to guess the exact meaning of **nasty**. However, the word **but** gives you an important clue. You know that **but** connects two opposite ideas. You also know that being wealthy is usually considered a good thing. Therefore, **nasty** must be a bad characteristic.

You can often also get a general meaning of nouns. Look at this example:

…from walls of water, to collapsing staircases, to falling smokestacks.

You do not need to know what a **smokestack** is in order to understand the basic idea here. You only need to know that something fell down and that it was probably something large.

There is probably is not enough information to figure out the exact meanings of the underlined words below. But you can get some information from the context. What can you infer about the meanings of these words? Write your ideas on the lines. What clues can you use in each sentence? Circle them.

1. In return,… he teaches her how to <u>spit</u> like a man.

   _____

2. The computer-generated special effects are simply <u>awesome</u>. There will be no doubt in your mind that the Titanic *is* sinking.

   _____

3. Jack is a poor but <u>bold</u> artist…

   _____

4. *Titanic* is an <u>epic</u> that women will love to cry at… Cameron has succeeded in making a wonderful romantic <u>epic</u>.

   _____

5. In addition, the main characters are <u>stereotypes</u>. Rose is beautiful and sweet. Jack is poor but honest. And Cal is thoroughly evil.

   _____

Step 3: Note Useful Information

1. **Readings 1, 2, and 3 contained facts and ideas that helped you to do Unit Task 1. Will Reading 4 be useful for doing Unit Task 2? Why? Why not?**

2. **Which of the following do you think will be helpful in Reading 4?**
   - the organization of the text
   - specific information about the movie *Titanic*
   - types of information that the writer chose to talk about
   - the writer's opinion about the movie

3. **Look back at the chart on page 71. What information did the writer of this movie review choose to include? Is there any information in the review that is not in that list?**

4. **Look at all the previous exercises for Reading 4. Which ones do you think give you the information that will help you to do Unit Task 2?**

F. Building Your Vocabulary

Below is a list of adjectives from Reading 4. Which ones are positive? Which are neutral? Which are negative? Check (✓) your answers. If you are not sure of the meaning of the words, look at the Vocabulary Strategy section on understanding the general meaning of unknown words (page 78). Complete the chart. An example has been done for you.

	POSITIVE	NEUTRAL	NEGATIVE
1. awesome	✓		
2. wonderful	✓		
3. undeveloped			✓
4. unrealistic			✓
5. old-fashioned		✓	
6. romantic	✓	✓	
7. amazing	✓	✓	
8. simple		✓	✓

G. Writing Your Ideas

Look at the writing topics below. Choose at least one and write about it.

1. Do you ever read movie reviews? Are you influenced by what movie critics think of a movie? Explain and give examples.

2. Do you like movies? Why or why not? What do you or don't you like about them? Explain and give examples to support your opinion.

READING 5: *"TITANIC* SINKS AGAIN (SPECTACULARLY)"

Step 1: Preview the Reading

1. **What kind of text is this? How do you know?**

2. **Look at the title. Can you guess the author's opinion about the movie?**

3. **Think about the organization of Reading 4. Where is the best place to look to find the author's general opinion? Scan that part of Reading 5 for the author's opinion. Did you find it? Did you guess correctly in question 2?**

4. **In addition to the author's opinion, what other information will probably be included in this reading?**

5. **Look back at the list of questions you wrote in your notebook for Unit Task 2. Which questions do you think this article may answer? Put a check mark (✓) next to them.**

Step 2: Read Closely

1. **Read the text. The first time you read, cover up the margin questions. Look for the answers to the questions you checked in your notebook. Write any answers that you find next to your questions.**

2. **Read the text again. Use the margin questions to help you.**

MOVIE REVIEW
Titanic Sinks Again (Spectacularly)
By KENNETH TURAN, TIMES FILM CRITIC

1   What does $200 million buy?—In the case of the movie *Titanic* the answer is "not enough." However, the answer is not, "Nothing." When you build a 775-foot, 90% scale model of the ship and sink it in a 17-million-gallon tank, you are going to get a lot of production value for your money, especially if your name is James Cameron.

2   More than that, at *Titanic*'s two-hour mark, when most films are ending, this giant film wakes up. With writer-director Cameron, a master of large-scale action-adventure films as director, the sinking of the ship is incredible to watch. But Cameron wants more than "oohs" and "aahs" from the audience. He has already made *The Terminator* and *Terminator 2*. He hopes that *Titanic* will be compared with romantic epics such as *Doctor Zhivago* and *Lawrence of Arabia*. Unfortunately, Cameron does not have the skill to make a movie classic such as these. In fact, just like the shipbuilders whose belief that the Titanic was unsinkable led to the disaster, James Cameron's pride has come close to destroying this film.

3   Seeing *Titanic* is a frustrating experience. Why? It is not because of the incredible budget or even because it recalls the death of so many people on the real ship.

What is really upsetting is James Cameron's belief that he has the ability to write the screenplay for this kind of movie. He is wrong. Cameron has written scripts in the past, but creating a realistic love story is different from writing funny dialog for Arnold Schwarzenegger.

4   Rather than a Hollywood classic, *Titanic* is an old Hollywood romance. It is a story without originality. Worse than that, many of the characters, especially the good-for-nothing Cal Hockley (played by Billy Zane) and Kathy Bates' Molly Brown are complete stereotypes. These characters are so bad that they ought to be studied in film schools as examples of how not to write for the movies.

5   One reason this movie is so long is that the story of the Titanic is framed by a modern-day story. This involves treasure hunter Brock Lovett (Bill Paxton), who is searching the Titanic's wreck for a fabulously expensive blue diamond called "The Heart of the Ocean."

6   What Lovett finds instead is a drawing of a young woman wearing the blue jewel. News of that find brings a phone call from 101-year-old Rose Dawson Calvert (Gloria Stuart), who says it's her in the drawing. Lovett invites Rose to join his expedition. Most of the

1. Say the words *ooh* and *aah*. Can you guess what they mean?

2. If you do not understand the word *frustrating* in paragraph 3, would you guess that it is a good thing or a bad thing?

3. The summary of the story begins in paragraph 5. Scan the next few paragraphs to find out where the summary ends.

4. What is the topic of paragraphs 7–8?

5. In paragraph 11, do you know what a *tumbleweed* is? Is it important to know the word?

6. What is the topic of paragraphs 12–13?

movie is her memory of what happened before, during and after the great ship went down.

7 Young Rose (now played by Kate Winslet) boarded the Titanic wearing a big hat and emotional handcuffs. "To me it was a slave ship," she recalls, "taking me to America in chains." In other words, her snooty mother Ruth DeWitt Bukater was forcing her into a loveless marriage with Cal Hockley, an arrogant, insensitive but wealthy snob.

8 Rose may be only 17, but she is amazingly knowledgeable. She makes comments about as yet unknown psychologist Sigmund Freud, an Austrian gentleman no one else on the ship has heard of. She also has unbelievable taste in art. While in Europe, she managed to buy paintings by still to be discovered painters such as Pablo Picasso, Edgar Degas and Claude Monet. Hockley of course, laughs at her choices. Clearly, this young woman deserves better than this ignorant fool, no matter how rich he is.

9 Enter Jack Dawson (Leonardo DiCaprio), a poor but talented artist who wins his ticket in a card game. Jack sees Rose and is taken by her beauty, and though another young man tells him that he has no chance to even meet her, Jack's not the kind of young man to give up easily.

10 Sure enough, despite the presence of 2,200 other passengers and crew, it's only Jack who is around

to save Rose when she considers suicide. Then, despite the best efforts of her mother Ruth (Frances Fisher) and Hockley's bad-tempered servant Spicer Lovejoy (David Warner), Jack and Rose get to know each other and fall in love. She teaches him manners and he teaches her how to spit like a man.

11 Both Winslet and DiCaprio are capable actors but their performances are hurt by some very silly dialog. "You could just call me a tumbleweed blowing in the wind," Jack says, adding later, "sooner or later the fire I love about you is going to burn out." The worst lines are given to Hockley and actress Kathy Bates' Molly Brown, who both have dialog more suitable for a comic book than a serious movie.

12 Finally, after so much time has passed that you begin to think that the iceberg will never appear, disaster strikes. Cameron is at his best here, and *Titanic's* closing hour is full of the incredibly dramatic and impressive sights, from walls of water flooding the grand dining room to the enormous ship itself going into the water vertically.

13 These kinds of complex and difficult scenes are done with so much self-confidence that it's understandable that the director thinks he can do it all. Yet, as Cameron sails his lonely ship toward greatness, he should realize he needs to bring a passenger with him. Preferably someone who can write.

Los Angeles Times, Friday Dec. 19, 1997

A. Checking Your Comprehension

Complete the chart with information from the movie review.

1. Good points about the movie _excellent director_

   _____

   specific examples _____

   _____

2. Criticisms of the movie _frustrating experience_

   _____

   specific examples _____

   _____

3. Comparisons with other movies _____

   _____

4. Overall opinion _____

   _____

B. Making Inferences

What inferences can you make about the reading? Answer these questions.

1. Does the writer think that *Doctor Zhivago* and *Lawrence of Arabia* are good movies?

2. What is the writer's opinion of *The Terminator* and *Terminator 2?*

3. What does the writer think about old Hollywood romances (paragraph 4)?

C. Topics for Discussion

Discuss the following questions with your classmates.

1. If you had read a review like this before you went to see a movie, would you go to see the movie? Why or why not?

2. Have you seen *Dr. Zhivago, Lawrence of Arabia* or the *Terminator* movies? Did you like them? Why or why not?

READING STRATEGY: Examining Organization

In looking at the organization of a reading it is important to be able identify the larger ideas that the author is trying to communicate. In this reading, the author's main purpose is to critique the film. This means we can guess that he will present good points and weak points of the film.

Does the reading divide clearly between positive and negative?

We also know that the author needs to summarize the story of the film. This information comes from our understanding of the type of text that it is.

When you read, you should be looking for these different parts.

---

1. **Make an organizational chart of Reading 5 similar to the one on page 77. Think about these questions.**

   1. How does this kind of text usually begin?

   2. How does it usually end?

   3. Which parts of the text summarize?

   4. Which parts are positive?

   5. Which are negative?

   6. Which are mixed?

2. **Compare the number of good points and the number of criticisms. What can we say about the author's overall feeling about the movie?**

READING STRATEGY: Understanding the Author's Tone

"Tone" refers to the manner in which the author writes. Writers can use words in special ways that show us their attitude or tone.

One common tone uses sarcasm. When a writer is being sarcastic, he or she criticizes but in an amusing way. The writer may make positive comments, but actually means the opposite. One way a writer does this is by making extreme statements. They are so extreme, that even if they are positive, we know that the writer is really criticizing. It is the difference between the writer's opinion and his words that makes us laugh.

We know that the writer of Reading 5 does not think that *Titantic* is a great film. He tells us this in statements such as:

Unfortunately, Cameron **does not have the skill** to make a movie classic such as these. In fact, just as the shipbuilders' belief that the Titanic was unsinkable led to the disaster, **James Cameron's pride has come close to destroying this film.**

The statements above are not sarcastic. The writer means exactly what he is saying. Compare them to the statements below, summarizing the plot. Even though he seems to be paying a compliment for the character of Rose, he is actually making fun of the script.

Rose may be only 17, but she is **amazingly knowledgeable**. She makes comments about as yet unknown psychologist Sigmund Freud, an Austrian gentleman **no one else on the ship has heard of**. She also **has unbelievable** taste in art. While in Europe, she managed to buy paintings by **still to be discovered painters** such as Pablo Picasso, Edgar Degas and Claude Monet. Hockley, of course, laughs at her choices. **Clearly, this young woman deserves better than this ignorant fool, no matter how rich he is**.

We interpret the author's words as sarcastic here because it is unusual for a 17-year-old to be knowledgeable about these things. The critic's words are too extreme to be believable, especially when he goes on to talk about Freud and the painters. In these statements, it is clear that he thinks it would be impossible for this young woman to know about them, and he is being sarcastic rather than complimentary.

---

3. **Read the comments below. Which ones show the author's tone to be funny or sarcastic? Check (✓) your answers.**

_____ 1. Young Rose (now played by Kate Winslet) boarded the Titanic wearing a big hat and emotional handcuffs.

_____ 2. Sure enough, despite the presence of 2,200 other passengers and crew, it's only Jack who is around to save Rose when she considers suicide.

_____ 3. Cameron is at his best here, and *Titanic's* closing hour is full of the incredibly dramatic and impressive sights, from walls of water flooding the grand dining room to the enormous ship itself going into the water vertically.

_____ 4. Yet, as Cameron sails his lonely ship toward greatness, he should realize he needs to bring a passenger with him. Preferably someone who can write.

_____ 5. When you build a 775-foot, 90% scale model of the ship and sink it in a 17-million-gallon tank, you are going to get a lot of production value for your money, especially if your name is James Cameron.

_____ 6. More than that, at *Titanic's* two-hour mark, when most films are ending, this giant film wakes up.

VOCABULARY STRATEGY:
More Practice on Looking for Information About Names

Information which describes people or places often comes right before or after the name. The information is sometimes set off by a comma or commas; however, this is not always the case.

Look at these examples. Which words or phrases describe the underlined names?

> He hopes that *Titanic* will be compared with romantic epics such as <u>Doctor Zhivago</u> and <u>Lawrence of Arabia</u>.

> Winslet plays <u>Rose DeWitt Bukater</u>, a rich Philadelphia girl returning to the United States from a vacation in Europe.

> You can't help wishing that <u>Kathy Bates</u>, as the nouveau riche Molly Brown, had a few more scenes.

> This involves treasure hunter Brock Lovett (Bill Paxton), who is searching the Titanic's wreck for a fabulously expensive blue diamond called <u>The Heart of the Ocean</u>.

How does the author identify these people? Does the identifying phrase come before the name, after the name, or both? Write the phrases on the lines.

1. Cal Hockley _____

2. Brock Lovett _____

3. Sigmund Freud _____

4. Pablo Picasso, Edgar Degas, Claude Monet _____

5. Jack Dawson _____

6. Spicer Lovejoy _____

Step 3: Note Useful Information

1. **Look back at the chart on page 71. What information did the writer of this movie review choose to include? Is there any information in the review that is not in that list? Are there any differences between Readings 4 and 5?**

2. **Look at the questions that you wrote for this reading. Which ones were answered? Look back and highlight any sections of Reading 5 that you think will help you to do Unit Task 2.**

F. Making Connections

Although Reading 4 is a generally positive review of the movie *Titanic* and Reading 5 is a generally negative review, they have many aspects in common. Complete the chart with similarities and differences. Find examples of each.

Similarities

Reading 4	Reading 5

Differences

Reading 4	Reading 5

G. Writing Your Ideas

Look at the writing topics below. Choose at least one and write about it.

1. Write about the similarities and differences between the two reviews. Give specific examples. The chart you completed in Making Connections will help you.

2. In your opinion, what knowledge and qualities does a person need to have in order to be a movie reviewer? Why? Explain.

Step 1: Preview the Reading

1. Look at the title. Can you guess what this text is about?

PREVIEWING STRATEGY:
Reading the Introduction and the Conclusion

If the title does not give you enough information on the topic of a text and there are no subtitles to help you, another way to find out about the text is by reading the first and last paragraphs. The first paragraph often introduces the topic and the last paragraph often summarizes the most important ideas.

Read the first paragraph of Reading 6. What can you guess the text will be about?

Read the last paragraph of Reading 6. What other information is probably included in the text?

---

2. Do you think this reading will help you with Unit Task 2? Why?

3. Look back at the list of questions you wrote in your notebook for Unit Task 2. Which questions do you think this reading may answer? Put a check mark (✓) next to them.

Step 2: Read Closely

1. Read the text. The first time you read, cover up the margin questions. Look for the answers to the questions you checked in your notebook. Write any answers that you find next to your questions.

2. Read the text again. Use the margin questions to help you.

READING 6

1. *Immediacy* is a very important concept in this reading. What word does it look like? If you do not understand the word now, keep it in mind as you read.

2. Does the example of *Psycho* help you to understand *immediacy*?

THE ART AND PSYCHOLOGY OF MOTION PICTURES

1   The most powerful characteristic of motion pictures is their immediacy. A film is not just a photograph of the real world, it also shows us what it is like to move about in it. No other art form touches its audience so directly. In order to understand the power of motion pictures, you must know about the art of motion pictures—how a film works—and its psychology—how it works on us.

2   In the early days of movies, movie viewers actually hid under their seats when they heard a train approaching on screen. Even moviegoers who have seen many movies shout aloud at the sudden appearance of Norman Bates in the famous shower scene in the movie *Psycho*. Film seems especially able to bring us close, to pull us in. A play or a novel may move us deeply, but they do not have the power of movies.

3. What do you think the writer is going to discuss next?

3　Motion is the key to understanding how a film's effects are achieved. On-screen motion is produced by one of three things: the movement of objects or persons in front of a motionless camera; the movement of the camera itself; the movement produced by editing the film; or some combination of these.

4. What is the main idea of this paragraph?

4　It is possible to make a film without moving the camera. The director can put the camera in one place and leave it there to film an entire production. Most of the earliest filmmakers did just this. The actors moved in these early films but the camera did not. The camera simply recorded the action. This type of film-making was soon criticized as "uncinematic." Thus, while it is possible to make a film without moving the camera, it is rarely done today.

5. What is the main idea of this paragraph?

5　It is also possible to make a film without editing. The British director, Alfred Hitchcock, experimented with this in *Rope* by shooting in one continuous take. Similarly, the character being filmed may remain stationary. American artist Andy Warhol once made an experimental film called *Empire* in which nothing moved. He simply left a camera filming in one spot in front of the Empire State Building for eight hours. The only thing that changed during that time was the light.

6. What does *however* signal here?

6　However, even when the actors move, the audience does not necessarily get a feeling of immediacy. When the only motion comes from the character being filmed, the effect is similar to an actor crossing a stage. The film simply records the action. This kind of motion is not likely to make audiences feel emotionally involved with the characters or the story. Rather, camera motion and editing create that involvement. It is these second and third kinds of motion that make movies different from other arts.

7. What kind of information do you predict will come after the first sentence in this paragraph?

7　There are two kinds of camera motion. The camera can remain in one place and change its relation to the character with different kinds of shots. The camera can also change its relation to the character by being moved from one place to another. For example, the opening segment of Orson Welles's *Citizen Kane* begins with a shot that moves slowly past a fence with a "No Trespassing" sign, through the garden, and then into the house of Charles Foster Kane. It stops only when it reaches the main character, Kane himself. The camera's position, like that of the audience, is that of an outsider. In another example, Hitchcock uses a moving camera to make audiences feel like insiders in *Vertigo*. Here both a tracking camera and a zoom lens are used to shoot down into a tower stairway. This shot makes the audience feel just like the man who, despite a great fear of heights, has gone to the top of a tower to save his lover.

8. Do you remember some of this technical vocabulary from Reading 1?

8　The technical capacities of the camera also make it possible for the director to control what the audience sees. The close-up, the zoom, the tracking camera let him make the audience focus on a particular aspect of a scene, even if they do not want to. These techniques and the ability to put the audience in the middle of the action on screen—on a running horse, inside a prison cell, in front of a judge and jury—help to explain film's immediacy.

9　Just as important to the art of film is the less obvious kind of "motion" produced by editing. Editing greatly increases the director's ability to control and use the elements of a story and the audience's relation to that story. A film is not acted out from beginning to end in front of a camera. It is constructed piece by piece, from separate "takes." The ability to edit film gives filmmakers another advantage that playwrights do not have. First, it frees the filmmaker from presenting a performance that takes place in one place at one time. Thus, for example, a director may edit a love scene shot in the studio against the background of street scenes shot separately "on location" in Paris or Rome, or may mix shots of a stuntman with shots of the famous actor supposedly doing the stunts.

10　Second, editing can break down individual actions into their parts. This makes it possible to show the same action as taking a long time or a very short time. In Sergio Leone's *Once Upon a Time in the West,* editing makes a two-minute wait at a train station seem to take a very long time. In the 1980's action thriller *Bullitt,* editing creates the fast-paced excitement of a car chase. Lastly, editing also makes it possible to mix two or more stories. Every movie fan is familiar with the suspense created by moving between the hero and the approaching "bad guy."

9. Do you understand *immediacy* well enough to explain it in your own words?

11　No matter what the director's goal is, film offers a number of different ways that he or she can control and direct the audience's response. It is the use of these capacities that makes film an art and is responsible for its greatest "special effect," its immediacy.

A. Checking Your Comprehension

Answer these questions about the reading. Write the answers in your notebook.

1. What does the author say makes a film powerful?
2. What are the three types of motion?
3. Are all three types of motion necessary to make a film?
4. Are all three types of motion usually used in a film?
5. What two types of motion does the author think are the most important?

B. Making Inferences

What inferences can you make about the reading? Answer the questions below.

1. Who do you think the author believes are more important for making a great movie, directors or actors? Why do you think so?
2. How does the author probably feel about Alfred Hitchcock and Orson Welles?

C. Topics for Discussion

Discuss the following questions with your classmates.

1. Do you agree that movies are the most powerful kind of art form?

2. Can you give an example of a movie you have seen, where you felt the film's immediacy? Explain.

3. Have you ever had the experience of not being able to watch a film? Can you explain this by using some of the information from Reading 6?

D. Reading Strategies

READING STRATEGY: Understanding the Use of Examples

Writers often give examples to help explain their ideas. Usually they make a point and then use the example to show that their point is true.

1. **Look back at the use of examples in Reading 6. Find these examples and explain the point the author is making by using them.**

    1. shower scene from *Psycho* _____

    2. *Rope* _____

    3. *Empire* _____

    4. opening segment from *Citizen Kane* _____

    5. tower scene from *Vertigo* _____

    6. train station scene from *Once Upon a Time in the West* _____

    7. car chase from *Bullitt* _____

READING STRATEGY: Looking for Guiding Sentences

"Guiding sentences" can help you to understand the organization of a reading and get ready for what is coming.

How does the underlined sentence help you to anticipate the information that will come next in the reading?

Motion is the key to understanding how a film's effects are achieved. <u>On-screen motion is produced by one of three things: the movement of objects or persons in front of a motionless camera; the movement of the camera itself; the movement produced by editing the film; or some combination of these.</u>

2. **Look at paragraph 7. Can you find a guiding sentence? Write it below.**

_____

Sometimes the topic of a paragraph is one of the main ideas of a reading, but not all paragraphs are equal in importance. Some paragraphs simply give examples or explain a main idea further. Therefore, in addition to knowing the topic of a paragraph you must understand its purpose and how it relates to the paragraphs that came before.

For example, look at paragraphs 1 and 2 in Reading 6.

What is the topic of paragraph 1? What are the topic and purpose of paragraph 2?

3. **The organization of Reading 6 might be diagrammed in this way. Study the diagram. Then look back at the reading and complete the chart by filling in the blank boxes with paragraph topics.**

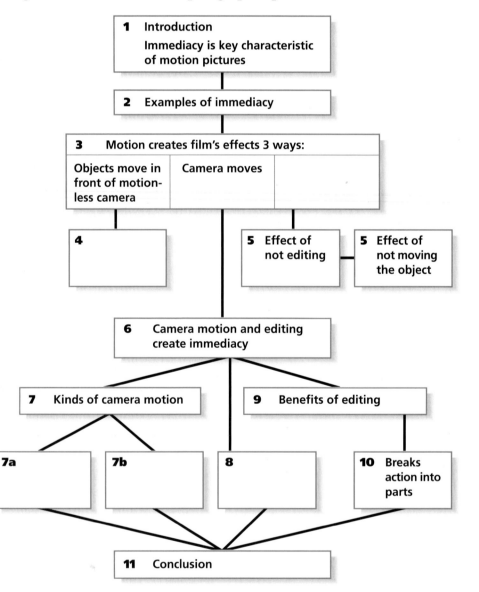

Look at the writing topics below. Choose at least one and write about it.

1. Write a composition comparing plays and movies, using some of the ideas in this reading.

2. Write about a movie that you have seen that had a powerful effect on you. Explain your feelings about the movie and how you think that movie achieved that effect on you.

UNIT TASK 2:
Reviewing a Movie

Find a movie that you want to watch and review. You may do this Unit Task individually or in pairs. If possible, try to review a movie that you can watch at home so that you can see it more than once if necessary. Before you watch the movie, review the readings and make a list of the elements that you may want to comment on. Not all of the elements will be present or noteworthy in every movie. However, think about each of them.

Complete the following steps in order to help you do Unit Task 2:

1. Make a list of the elements that make up a movie.

   a. _____

   b. _____

   c. _____

   d. _____

   e. _____

   f. _____

   g. _____

   h. _____

   i. _____

2. Look back at the readings and find information about what makes a movie good. Write some of the ideas below.

   _____

   _____

   _____

   _____

3. Now watch the movie and make notes of the elements that you notice. Compare your notes with your partner. Decide which elements you feel are the most important in this movie.

_____

_____

_____

_____

4. Look back at the readings and the exercises and make a list of the content that <u>must</u> be included in a movie review. Add any other content that you feel will be important in a review of this movie. Then make an outline similar to the outline on page 74.

5. Finally, prepare a written or oral report for your class.

PART C EXPANSION ACTIVITIES

Applying Your Knowledge

1. Read other movie reviews and critique them, based on the information you have learned about movies and about writing movie reviews.

2. Watch the movie *Titanic*. Do you agree with either of the movie reviews? Explain.

3. Watch one of the movies that was mentioned in the readings. Do you think that it deserves to be called a classic? Why or why not.

4. Read the short screenplay on page 208 in the Additional Readings section. In groups, decide on an appropriate series of shots and camera angles.

The Electronic Link

The following is the address for the homepage of the Academy of Motion Picture Arts and Sciences. This is the organization that gives out the Academy Awards.

http://www.oscar.com/

The following are two sites where you can find movie reviews.

http://www.movielinemag.com/

http://radiofree.com/

The site below is one where you can send your own movie review.

http://www.geocities.com/Hollywood/Academy/5218/

For More Information

Making Movies Work: Thinking Like a Filmmaker
Jon Boorstin
Los Angeles: Silman James Press, 1995.

How Movies Work
Bruce F. Kawin
Los Angeles: University of California Press, 1992.

Understanding Movies
Luigi D. Gianetti, et al.
Englewood Cliffs, NJ: Prentice Hall, 1998.

Making Movies
Sidney Lumet
New York: Vintage Books, 1996.

See the Additional Readings for this unit on pages 206–211.

Essay Questions

Choose one of the topics below and write an essay about it.

1. Has the information you have learned about how movies are made and how they achieve their effects changed how you feel about movies? Do you think that you will enjoy movies more or less than you did before? Give reasons for your answers.

2. A famous director once said, "Cinema is truth at 24 frames a second and every time you cut, you lie." What did he mean? Do you agree or disagree? Why?

Evaluating Your Progress

Think about the skills and strategies that you used in this unit. Check (✓) the correct boxes.

	NEVER	SOMETIMES	OFTEN	ALWAYS
1. I was able to use my background knowledge to predict the information that I would find in a reading.	☐	☐	☐	☐
2. When I previewed, I thought about where a reading came from and what I knew about the topic.	☐	☐	☐	☐
3. I was able to predict the purpose of a reading.	☐	☐	☐	☐
4. I was able to guess the general meaning of unknown words.	☐	☐	☐	☐
5. I was able to use my general knowledge to guess the meaning of unknown words.	☐	☐	☐	☐
6. I was able to use examples to understand difficult ideas.	☐	☐	☐	☐
7. I was able to use subtitles and formatting to make predictions about the reading.	☐	☐	☐	☐
8. I looked for guiding sentences as I read.	☐	☐	☐	☐
9. I was able to use synonyms to understand new words.	☐	☐	☐	☐
10. I thought about parts of speech when I was trying to figure out the meaning of unknown words.	☐	☐	☐	☐

Setting Your Reading Goals

1. Choose three items from the list on page 96 that you would like to improve. Write them below.

   Goal #1 _____

   Goal #2 _____

   Goal #3 _____

2. Look back at your reading goals from Unit 1 on page 45. Are you moving toward these goals?

IN THIS UNIT

Reading Strategies

- Using charts, graphs, and tables
- Understanding reference words
- Recognizing the important ideas of a text
- Understanding different levels of information

Strategies for Unknown Vocabulary

- Deciding when to use the dictionary
- Understanding dictionary entries
- Choosing the correct meaning
- Using general knowledge to guess the meaning of unknown words
- Understanding the meaning of suffixes
- Recognizing related words and parts of speech

Money Makes the World Go 'Round (Or Does It?)

Think About It

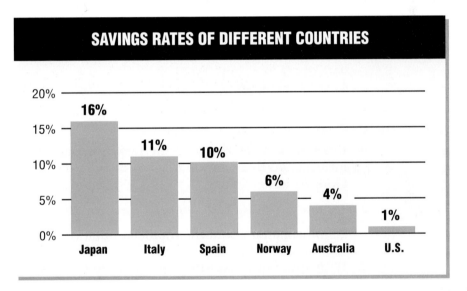

SAVINGS RATES OF DIFFERENT COUNTRIES

Discuss these questions with your classmates.

1. In which country do people save the most?
2. In which country do people save the least?
3. Do you think that it is important to save money? Why or why not?

Looking Ahead in Unit Three

Look at each of the readings in this unit. Match the readings in the unit with the types of readings listed below. Write the reading numbers on the lines. How do you know which kind of reading each one is? (Some types of readings appear more than once in this unit.)

READING NUMBER(S)

1. a newspaper article _____

2. a magazine article _____

3. a chapter from a book _____

4. a magazine column _____

Looking at the Unit Tasks

This unit has two tasks. The first one occurs after Reading 3 on page 125. You will do the second one after Reading 6 on page 145. Look for the two Unit Tasks and write their titles below.

Unit Task 1 _____

Unit Task 2 _____

PART A   UNIT TASK 1: GIVING FINANCIAL ADVICE

Identify the Information You Need

1. **Read the instructions for Unit Task 1 on page 125. Think about the information that you will need to do it. You will need two different kinds of information:**

   1. how to use and save money wisely (money management)

   2. information about the financial situation of the Pandit family

2. **Write questions that will help you to do Unit Task 1 on the lines below.**

   QUESTIONS ABOUT MONEY MANAGEMENT IN GENERAL

   1. _____?

   2. _____?

   3. _____?

   4. _____?

   5. _____?

6. _____?

7. _____?

8. _____?

9. _____?

10. _____?

3. Compare your questions with your classmates' questions. Are there any questions that you want to add to your list? Copy your final list of questions into your notebook.

4. Now look ahead to Readings 1–3. Which of them might give you the answers to each question? Draw a chart like the one on page 70, exercise 3, into your notebook. Write the question numbers and the reading numbers on the lines.

READING 1: "BASIC MONEY RULES"

Step 1: Preview the Reading

1. Where do you think this reading comes from?

2. Who wrote it?

3. Look at the title and the first sentence. Who do you think the author was writing the text for?

PREVIEWING STRATEGY: Noticing Illustrations

One good way to preview a reading is to look at the pictures or illustrations. Illustrations can be photographs, drawings, charts, or graphs. They often have titles or explanations that can also give you important information.

Look at this reading. What kind of illustrations does it have?

What do the explanations under the pictures tell you?

---

4. Look back at the list of questions you wrote in your notebook for Unit Task 1. Which questions do you think this article may answer? Put a check mark (✓) next to them.

1. **Read the text. The first time you read, cover up the margin questions. Look for the answers to the questions you checked in your notebook. Write any answers that you find next to your questions.**

2. **Read the text again. Use the margin questions to help you.**

   Note: This reading introduces some vocabulary that will be useful later in the unit. As you read more about money you will understand more vocabulary.

READING 1

BASIC MONEY RULES

1 To get from where you are to where you want to be, financially, you will need to use some basic money rules. The first rule is that in order to build a fortune, you must put your money to work. Earning a high salary does not do much good unless some of the money also starts making money. If you save just a little from each paycheck, eventually this money will earn more than you do—that is, if you give it enough time.

SHORTCUTS DO NOT WORK

1. What formatting feature helps you to guess the topic of each section?

2. Can you state in your own words the second rule of money management?

2 Shortcuts to financial success seldom work. In other words, there is no quick way to get rich. That leads to the second rule. You gain wealth by combining money with time and growth. All three must be present for lasting results. There are no exceptions to this basic rule. Unless you are going to inherit a lot of money when a rich family member dies, you need to get some of your money working for you.

3. If you do not understand *nest-egg*, read to the end of the paragraph. Do you understand it now?

3 Money that is working for you is the only reliable way to build a nest-egg. All you need is an average salary and enough self-control to save regularly. The discipline to continue saving a little money every month is more important than the amount that you save. Even just a few dollars saved regularly will eventually grow to be a large amount.

THE IMPORTANCE OF TIME

4. What example does the author give? Why?

4 Money and time work together. More time allows less money to grow into a large amount. Money that you have saved, however, doesn't double overnight. Just as apple trees need time to develop before they produce fruit, savings need to mature for a period of time before they start producing.

Table 4.1 illustrates the time miracle. It shows how much money you need to save each month at different ages in order to have $100,000 in today's dollars at age 65 if you receive 6% interest per year.

Table 4.1
THE MIRACLE OF TIME

Monthly Amount Needed to be Saved to Have $100,000 at Age 65 @ 6%

Age	
25 years	$49.96
30 years	69.84
35 years	99.06
40 years	143.58
45 years	215.35
50 years	342.15
55 years	607.17

5. What does this paragraph refer to?

5 Notice that you need to save over four times more money at age forty-five than at age twenty-five in order to reach the same goal. By age fifty-five, with only ten years left, you need twelve times more! No wonder so many people in their fifties say, "Why didn't someone tell me to start saving when I was twenty?"

THE IMPORTANCE OF GROWTH

6. What two ideas does *so* connect?

6 Money and growth work together because the money that you invest doubles, and then redoubles at a speed set by the rate of interest it receives. For most people, getting rich quickly through a high interest rate isn't possible. However, the return must not be too low because prices usually go up over time, so the interest rate must be enough to keep up with price inflation.

7. If you do not understand *compound*, look ahead. Where will you probably find out what it means?

7 To get ahead, your money must earn more than average price increases. A higher rate of return means higher profits. For instance, $10,000 earning 3% interest grows to only $18,180 in twenty years; but $10,000 earning 9% grows to $106,409 in twenty years. Compounding at the higher rate produces nearly six times more money (from $18,180 to $106,409). Examine Table 4.2 to see the results of saving only $25 per month ($300 a year) at four different rates of compound return: 3%, 6%, 9%, and 12%.

Table 4.2
RESULTS OF SAVING $25 PER MONTH

	Rate of Compound Interest			
	3%	**6%**	**9%**	**12%**
20 years	$8,228	$11,609	$16,822	$24,979
30 years	$14,605	$25,238	$46,112	$88,248
40 years	$23,209	$50,036	$117,911	$297,061

8. What does this paragraph refer to?

8 Notice that saving $25 per month at 6% produces $50,036 in forty years, but at 9% the total grows to $117,911 and at 12% it reaches an incredible $297,061! Not bad for a $12,000 investment.

COMPOUND INTEREST AND THE RULE OF 72

9. Does this paragraph tell you what *compound* means?

10. Can you guess the meaning of *principal*?

9 Your money grows in a savings account by earning compound interest. This means that interest is added to your principal and the total amount will earn interest for the next time period. The time period for compounding may be daily, weekly, monthly, quarterly or annually.

10 The Rule of 72 is an easy way to predict money growth on compound rates of return. This rule shows how many years are needed for a sum of money to double at various rates. Simply divide 72 by the interest rate such as 6%. The answer gives you the number of years needed for the principal to double.

For example:
$500 earning 6% doubles to $1,000 in 12 years (72 ÷ 6%) =12
$500 earning 12% doubles to $1,000 in 6 years (72 ÷ 12%) = 6

11. What is the purpose of this example?

11 The eighteenth century American, Benjamin Franklin, understood how money grows over time. When he died in 1791, he left $5,000 to the city of Boston. He told them that they could not touch it for 100 years. By 1891, the $5,000 had grown to $322,000. The city built a school with some of the money, but also followed Ben's wishes to leave $92,000 for another hundred years. By 1960 this fund had grown to $1,400,000! Although you probably won't save your money for a hundred years, compounding can still work miracles for you.

A. Checking Your Comprehension

Answer the questions about the readings on the lines below.

1. What three things create wealth?

   _____ plus _____ plus _____

2. If you want to increase your wealth, what should you do, according to this reading?

   _____

3. State the rule of 72 in your own words.

   _____

4. Which is better, saving a large amount of money over a short time, or small amounts of money over a long time? Why?

   _____

B. Making Inferences

1. **Why did Benjamin Franklin tell the city of Boston that they could not use his money for 100 years?**

2. **Which of these do you think is the author's most important point in this text? Circle your answer.**

   a. You should save as much money as possible starting from the time that you are young.

   b. Even if you only save small amounts of money, eventually you can have a large amount.

   c. You need a lot of money to be happy.

C. Topics for Discussion

Discuss the following questions with your classmates.

1. Are you good at saving money? What is a good place or way to save it? What is a good rate of interest to receive these days?

2. What are some advantages and disadvantages of keeping your money in a savings account?

3. Besides savings, what are some other ways that people can make their money work for them?

READING STRATEGY: Using Charts, Graphs, and Tables

Charts, graphs and tables can help you understand the information in a reading because they often give you the same information in a visual form. It is sometimes easier to understand the chart or graph than the words.

Look at Table 4.1 on page 103 in Reading 1. Find the paragraph in the text that this table illustrates and draw a line from the table to it. Which is easier for you to understand, the table or the words?

Which paragraph does Table 4.2 on page 104 illustrate?

1. Look at the graph below. What does it illustrate? How do you know?

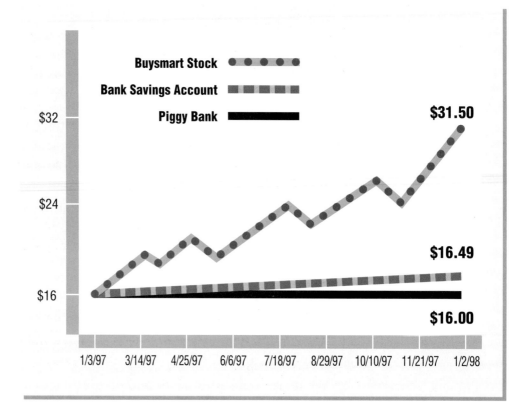

In Unit 2 you learned about words that take the place of other words. You looked at personal pronouns (**I, you, he, she, we, they**), as well as the words **this** and **that.**

Sometimes, the reference words **this** and **it** may refer to larger phrases or whole ideas instead of single words or simple noun phrases.

The word **this** often occurs before a noun, as in the sentence below.

When you save just a little from each paycheck, eventually **this money** will earn more than you do—that is, if you give **it** enough time.

What does the phrase **this money** refer to? What does **it** refer to? What does **a little** mean?

Sometimes **this** occurs alone, as in the following example:

Your money grows in a savings account by earning compound interest. **This** means that interest is added to your principal where it will earn interest for the next time period.

What does **this** refer to here? Does it refer to a word or an idea?

2. **What does *this* or *it* refer to in these sentences? Look back at the paragraphs in the reading to find the answers and write them below.**

1. That is, if you give <u>it</u> enough time. (paragraph 1) _____

2. Notice that saving $25 per month at 6% produces $50,036 in forty years; but at 9% the total grows to $117,911 and at 12% <u>it</u> reaches an incredible $297,061! (paragraph 8) _____

3. <u>This rule</u> shows how many years are needed for a sum to double at various rates. (paragraph 10) _____

4. By 1960, <u>this fund</u> had grown to $1,400,000! (paragraph 11)

   _____

5. He told them that they could not touch <u>it</u> for 100 years. (paragraph 11)_____

VOCABULARY STRATEGY: Deciding When to Use the Dictionary

Sometimes you can guess the meaning of unknown words by using other information in the context. Even if you can only get a general idea of the meaning, it is often good enough. However, sometimes a reading contains new words that are so important that you need to know their exact meanings.

There is no absolute rule for deciding when a word is very important and when it is not. However, when the word occurs several times in the same reading or it appears in an important phrase or sentence, then you should probably look it up in the dictionary.

Try not to look up a word the first time that you see it. Instead, try to get a general idea of what the word means. If you finish reading the text for the first time and still do not understand the word, then look it up in an English-only dictionary.

For example, you can think about the word **earn** this way:

How many times is **earn** *used in the text?* **Earn** *(or a form of* **earn***) occurs about eight times in Reading 1. How is it used?*

Earning a high salary does not do much good unless some of the money also starts making money. If you save just a little from each paycheck, eventually this money will **earn** more than you do…

From this example and the number of times that it is used, I can see that **earn** *is an important word directly related to money and money management. I want to make sure that I know exactly what it means, so I will look it up in the dictionary.*

1. **Now that you have read the text at least once, think about the words below. Which of the words do you think will be important for doing Unit Task 1? Put a checkmark (✓) next to them.**

discipline	get ahead	goal	grow	wealth
inherit	invest	mature	nest-egg	principal
produce	reliable	return	save	average
miracle	monthly	annually	salary	paycheck
double	rate of return	inflation	compound	financial

Of the list of important words you've checked, are there any that you think you should look up in the dictionary?

VOCABULARY STRATEGY: Understanding Dictionary Entries

A good dictionary tells you the meaning of a word and gives you a lot of other information as well. Here are some of the kinds of information that a dictionary can give you:

• the pronunciation

• parts of speech (noun, verb, adjective, adverb, etc.)

- grammatical information

- synonyms and/or antonyms

- example phrases or sentences to help you understand the meaning of a word and how it is used in a sentence

- other words it is commonly used with (collocations)

Every dictionary has its own system of notations and abbreviations. The introduction to the dictionary usually explains what these are. It is important for you to learn the system that your dictionary uses.

2. **The example below is from the *Oxford ESL Dictionary*. Can you figure out its system by looking at these entries?**

3. **What does each example of words, numbers, letters or symbols tell you?**

1. /ˈɪntrɪst/ _____

2. ~ _____

3. **1 2 3 etc** _____

4. *words in italics* _____

5. [C] _____

6. **in·ter·est¹   in·ter·est²** _____

7. *work in the ~(s) of humanity.* _____

8. *His story ~ed everyone in the room.* _____

Many words have more than one meaning. Therefore, it is very important to be careful when you use the dictionary.

First, if the word is used more than once in the reading, look at the word in at least two contexts. Is it the same part of speech in both places? If not, it is not the same word in both cases (although the two words may be closely related). Then look in the dictionary. Look for the entries that correspond to the parts of speech of the words in the reading.

Read through the definitions in order to choose the one that makes the most sense. Look back at the text. Does this meaning make sense in both contexts? If not, you may have the wrong definition, or the word might be used differently in each place. If the word is used differently, there should be another definition that fits the other context. Look for another meaning that fits the context.

Look at the word **interest**. Find at least two examples of **interest** in Reading 1. Is it the same part of speech in both places? What part of speech is it?

Read the two dictionary entries for **interest** on page 109. Which entry are you going to use? Which definition makes the most sense for your example sentences?

4. **Now look up these words in an English-only dictionary. Which definition makes the most sense for the context(s) in Reading 1?**

   1. invest _____

   2. return _____

   3. principal _____

   4. produce _____

Step 3: Note Useful Information

What kind of general information will a family who needs financial help need? Look back at Reading 1. Find useful rules for family money management. Underline them. The reading also gives many examples. Will the examples be useful for Unit Task 1? Why or why not?

F. Building Your Vocabulary

A word web is a diagram that shows how words are related. Look back at the word web in Unit 2 on page 55. In your notebook, begin another word web for the money management vocabulary in the previous exercises. Leave room to add additional useful money management vocabulary. You can begin with the word web below and add to it, or you can use your own ideas.

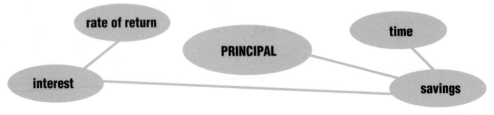

Look at the writing topics below. Choose at least one and write about it.

1. How do you feel about having a lot of money? Is it important to you? Why or why not? Explain.

2. How do you manage your money? Do you save it all, do you spend it all, or do you do something in between?

3. If you unexpectedly received a large amount of money (for example, $10,000) what would you do with it in order to make it "work for you"?

READING 2: "LIVING DANGEROUSLY"

Step 1: Previewing the Reading

1. **Look at the title of the article. What do you think it is about? Explain it in your own words.**

2. **One important word can be used to explain the topic of the article. What word do you think tells you the most about the topic of the article? Scan the text for that word. Underline it every time it occurs. Did you guess correctly? Was the word you chose closely related to the topic of the article?**

3. **Look back at the list of questions you wrote in your notebook for Unit Task 1. Which questions do you think this article may answer? Put a check mark (✓) next to them.**

Step 2: Read Closely

1. **Read the text. The first time you read, cover up the margin questions. Look for the answers to the questions you checked in your notebook. Write any answers that you find next to your questions.**

2. **Read the text again. Use the margin questions to help you.**

READING 2

FINANCE

Living Dangerously
Or the Risks of Spending Your Life in Debt

by Christine Dugas
USA TODAY

1. What is the purpose of this paragraph?

1 ATLANTA — After Chris Colizzi got married in 1984, he started using credit cards to pay for things when he didn't have enough money. He used them for things such as appliances for his new home, and for vacations. By 1996, Colizzi had

2. Is there enough information to guess the meaning of *bankruptcy* (paragraph 1)? If not, continue reading.

3. What does *this* refer to in paragraph 2?

4. What does the formatting tell you about USA Today/CNN?

5. What does *this* refer to in paragraph 4?

6. Does paragraph 5 give you any more information about the word *bankruptcy?* If not, is it important enough to look up in the dictionary?

7. What is the purpose of paragraph 6?

8. What three social problems are mentioned in paragraph 7? How are they similar?

about a dozen credit cards and $47,000 in card charges and personal loans. Financial stress from the growing debt helped to cause his divorce. In the end, Colizzi filed for bankruptcy.

2 "A lot of credit was offered to me, and I took it," says Colizzi, 33, a salesman in Geneva, N.Y. "I wasn't worried because I was able to make the minimum payments that the credit card companies asked for each month." With the economy going well and unemployment low, many Americans believe they, too, can handle their increasing debts. Credit card companies continue giving them credit and this makes them more confident about their ability to spend more. But too many people today have no safety net. A USA TODAY/CNN Gallup Survey of 1,006 adults found that more than a third — 35% — say they have no money put aside in case of a financial setback, such as losing a job.

3 That means millions of people are living dangerously with credit card debts that are often more than their salaries for the year. This year, U.S. credit card holders are expected to pay $62.5 billion or $568 per household in interest charges alone. And there is plenty of room for people to take on more debt. The unused portion of bank card limits totals an incredible $1.5 trillion, or $13,636 for every household.

4 Even those who pay every month may be in trouble. Like Colizzi, nearly a third of those surveyed in the USA TODAY poll — 27% — said they paid the minimum, or less, the last time they paid their credit card bills. This is exactly what credit card companies want. If card holders make only minimum payments on their bills, it could take a lifetime to get out of debt. For example, if you only made the minimum monthly payments on a $10,000 bill with a 17% interest rate, it would take 50 years to pay off the entire amount, says Gerri Detweiler, author of *The Ultimate Credit Handbook.*

5 Unfortunately, these numbers are not exaggerated. Hundreds of callers to USA TODAY's Debt Buster HotLine on Wednesday complained about the amount of debt they have, sometimes as much as $40,000. Others said even though they have good jobs and steady incomes, their credit card debt makes it impossible for them to buy a house. Today, even though the economy is good, personal bankruptcies are increasing. There are many reasons for this, including the economy itself, experts say.

6 "I don't hesitate to spend," says Kevin Campbell of Atlanta, a sales manager for a software company. "The economy and low interest rates make me feel more confident." Campbell has a good job and pays more than the monthly minimum on his credit card bills. But recently, he was turned down for a debit card because he owed so much money. "I was amazed we'd managed to build up that much debt," he says.

7 Consumers of every age and income level have debt problems. "The problem is spread all over," says Durant Abernethy, president of the National Foundation for Consumer Credit. "It's like other social problems, such as divorce or alcoholism.

9. Which word introduces the conclusion in paragraph 9?

Every group is affected."

8 "Unfortunately, many consumers are using credit cards to meet everyday expenses," says Paul Richard, vice president of the National Center for Financial Education. "If they lose their jobs, they use their cards to buy food and pay the rent."

9 Ultimately, consumers must take responsibility for living within limits, Abernethy says. Colizzi says he had no idea how to manage his money when he got his first credit cards. "I blame myself," he says. "But I didn't realize what I was doing. Things just got out of control."

A. Checking Your Comprehension

1. **Complete the following application for bankruptcy, based on the information in Reading 2.**

Application for Bankruptcy

Name _Christopher Colizzi_   Age_____

Marital Status   ☐ single ☐ married ☐ divorced ☐ widowed

Occupation_____

Amount of Debt_____

Explain why it is necessary for you to file for bankruptcy.

_____

_____

_____

---

2. **Find the number that goes with each description from Reading 2.**

1. the number of people in the USA Today/CNN Gallup survey   _____

2. the percentage of people who paid the minimum or less the last time they paid their credit card bill   _____

3. the percentage of people who have not saved any money   _____

4. the total amount of interest that credit card holders in the US will pay this year   _____

5. the total amount of money on the unused portion of bank card limits   _____

B. Making Inferences

What inferences can you make about the reading? Answer the questions below.

1. How has Chris Colizzi's attitude toward money changed since 1984?

2. Who benefits when consumers get more in debt?

3. Why is it bad to use credit cards to pay everyday expenses?

4. Why would it take 50 years to pay off a $10,000 bill if you only make the minimum payment each month?

C. Topics for Discussion

Discuss the following questions with your classmates.

1. Should the government do anything about the growing amount of credit card debt? What could they do?

2. Do you think that credit card companies are to blame for this problem? If so, what should they do differently?

3. Some people think that being in debt is a terrible thing. Do you agree? Why or why not? Is there any situation in which it might be good? Explain.

D. Reading Strategies

READING STRATEGY: Recognizing the Important Ideas of a Text

A text usually has one or more important ideas. These ideas are supported by details. It is important to be able to distinguish the important ideas from the details.

The following statement is an important point. It is one of the ideas that the author would like readers to remember.

It takes a long time to get out of debt if you only make the minimum payments.

The following statement is a detail. It is an example that helps readers to understand the important idea above.

If you pay $200 a month, it will take 50 years to pay off a $10,000 debt with 17% interest.

---

1. **Which of these ideas do you think are important ideas in this article? Which are details? Check (✓) your answers.**

	IMPORTANT IDEA	DETAIL
1. A USA TODAY/CNN Gallup survey found that 35% of the people it surveyed have no money put aside.	_____	✓
	_____	_____
2. Credit card debts often can cause other problems.	_____	_____

3. Financial stress from growing debt caused Chris Colizzi's divorce. ____ ____

4. Kevin Campbell didn't hesitate to spend because the economy and low interest rates made him feel more confident. ____ ____

5. Many Americans take on too much credit card debt and put themselves at risk financially. ____ ____

6. Many people are not worried about their debt. ____ ____

7. Chris Colizzi wasn't worried because he was able to make the minimum payments that the credit card companies asked for each month. ____ ____

8. Kevin Campbell was turned down for a debit card because he owed too much money already. ____ ____

9. Many people have no extra savings in case of a financial difficulty. ____ ____

10. Too much debt can make it impossible for a person to buy a home. ____ ____

2. **Compare your answers with a classmate's. Is it always clear which ideas are main ideas and which are details?**

READING STRATEGY:
Understanding Different Levels of Information

A well-written text can be organized like a pyramid. Look at the example below.

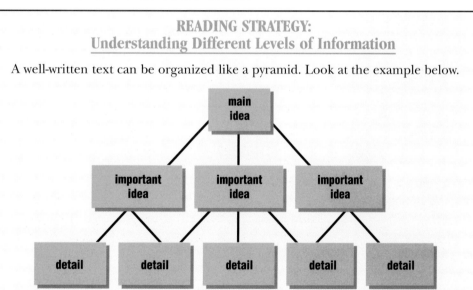

A text does not have to be organized exactly this way. For example, there may be more than one main idea, especially if the text is very long. However, it is still useful to keep this structure in mind as you read. It will help you to keep thinking about the relative importance of the ideas.

---

3. Look at Exercise 1. Of the important ideas, is there one idea that seems to include all of the others? Which one is it? What can we say about this idea?

4. Now, on another piece of paper, copy the main idea at the top and put the nine remaining ideas into a pyramid like the one in the box above. Remember to put the important ideas under the main idea, and then the details at the bottom. Can you figure out which details fit under each important idea? (Hint: There are three important ideas.)

E. Strategies for Unknown Vocabulary

VOCABULARY STRATEGY:
More Practice Choosing the Correct Meaning

A dictionary usually gives an example sentence or phrase for each meaning of a word. The example sentence can be very useful. If you are not sure which meaning is the one you need, the example sentence often gives you more clues.

Look these words up in the dictionary. Which definition makes sense in Reading 2?

word	part of speech	example sentence or phrase	definition
1. charge(s)			
2. credit			
3. bill(s)			
4. file (for bankruptcy)			
5. handle			

Step 3: Note Useful Information

Even when a text has one main idea, that idea may not be useful for your purpose. The ideas which are most important for your purpose might be secondary ideas or even details for the original author.

Think about Unit Task 1. Look back at the list of important ideas and details in the first Reading Strategy exercise on page 114. Which ideas do you think will be most useful for your purpose? Write them in your notebooks. You may need to add others that are not on this list.

F. Building Your Vocabulary

Look back through the reading. Find at least five new money management words to add to the word web in your notebook. Write a sentence using each word.

G. Writing Your Ideas

Look at the writing topics below. Choose at least one and write about it.

1. Do you have a credit card? What do you use it for? How do you pay your bills? Do you think that you should manage your finances differently?

2. If you do not have a credit card, would you like to have one? Why or why not? Do you think that credit cards are a good idea? Why or why not?

H. Making Connections

1. **Readings 1 and 2 both talk about *interest*. Does this word have the same meaning in both readings? How are they the same or different?**

2. **If a person wants to be in a good financial situation, which is more important, taking care of his or her savings, or taking care of his or her debts? Why do you think so?**

Step 1: Preview the Reading

1. **If you want to find out quickly what this article is about, which parts of the text will you look at? Write a one-sentence prediction of what you think this article will be about.**

   _____

2. **Scan the list of family expenses on page 120 to answer these questions.**

   a. What is this family's annual income?

   b. What is the total of their annual expenses?

   c. What is their single largest expense?

3. **Look back at the list of questions you wrote in your notebook for Unit Task 1. Which questions do you think this article may answer? Put a check mark (✓) next to them.**

Step 2: Read Closely

1. **Read the text. The first time you read, cover up the margin questions. Look for the answers to the questions you checked in your notebook. Write any answers that you find next to your questions.**

2. **Read the text again. Use the margin questions to help you.**

READING 3

1. Can you describe Ritu in your own words?

A Family in Financial Crisis

1 As the ice-skater finishes her routine, the audience begins to clap and then to cheer. Finally, they rise to their feet to show their appreciation for a brilliant performance. Is this unusual? Not really—except for the age of the skater. Ritu Pandit is just ten years old. Experts are already predicting that she'll go on to be one of the greatest skaters the world has ever seen.

2 Ritu's dad, Rajiv ("Ray"), 35, is an architect, and her mother Maribel, 31, is a homemaker. They are still amazed by their gifted daughter. Ray is from India and has lived in the United States for about fifteen years. His wife was born in the Dominican Republic. They had

2. What does the word *however* signal in paragraph 2?

3. What is the main idea of paragraph 3?

4. What does the first sentence tell you about what's coming in paragraph 3?

5. What does *it* refer to in paragraph 4?

no idea that their first-born daughter would be so talented. In fact, neither of them has ever ice-skated. Maribel says, "There aren't many ice rinks in India or the Dominican Republic." However, Ritu's talent became clear when she went skating with a friend's family at the age of four. She begged to take lessons and quickly progressed. Within two years she was easily able to do moves that children twice her age found difficult. Now, at the age of ten, she has five years before she can compete at the senior level, although she could probably beat many of the senior women right now.

3   When it became clear that Ritu needed private lessons, Ray and Maribel readily agreed. They hired a private coach at $250 a month. They also hired a tutor to help her with her school work because she often misses school when she goes to competitions.

4   The next step will be to send Ritu away to continue her lessons. Ray explains, "Her coach here in Sweet Springs is good, but even she says that Ritu will need a world-class coach if she is going to achieve her full potential as a skater. That means sending her to live at one of the major ice-skating training facilities. There isn't a good enough coach for her in the whole state of Kansas." The Pandits have now decided that Maribel will go to Detroit with Ritu. Ray will stay behind with their two younger children. "It's not a great solution," he says, "but there really was no good answer. We didn't want Ritu to live with another family, and we also didn't want to deny her this opportunity."

5   Having such a talented child has both benefits and difficulties. Financially, it can be especially difficult. Not only is there the cost of private lessons, but also the cost of traveling to competitions and paying for equipment and costumes. In addition, Maribel sometimes has to hire a companion to accompany her daughter to competitions because Maribel cannot always go along. The Pandits have two other children to take care of.

6   When Maribel goes to live with Ritu in Detroit, there will be a big increase in their expenses. They estimate that it will cost about $500 to rent a small apartment and $300 a month to pay for and run another car. There will also be heavy travel expenses because Maribel and Ritu will go home to visit at least once a month. Ray thinks that travel alone could cost $600 a month. It is easy to see how the family's expenses could get out of hand.

7   Ray makes about $95,000 a year as an architect. He and his family have always lived the good life. He drives a 1995 Lexus (value: $28,000). He built their beautiful home, but pays heavily for the mortgage ($3,000 a month). "When you're an architect, people look at the kind of house you live in. If your house is a place that everyone envies, they have more confidence that you can do the same for them."

8   Ray's lifestyle is dangerous for his family's financial situation. He has no life insurance. So if anything happens to him, his family has no financial protection. Last year, he didn't have enough money to pay his taxes and still owes the government $8,000. Maribel's father, Arturo, lives with them, and they pay all of his expenses. His medicine costs $200 monthly, and they spend about $300 a month on calls to their families in India and the Dominican Republic.

9   That would be all right if the Pandits didn't have so many other bills. Recently, Ray sent $5,000 to relatives in the Dominican Republic recovering from a hurricane. Then came $5,000 in home-improvement bills, followed by medical bills for Arturo and Maribel. Ray borrowed $10,000 from his sister and still has to work 14 hours a day to make all the payments.

10   The question now is, how will the Pandits be able to pay for Ritu's ice-skating career. Professional ice-skaters can make a lot of money, but an Olympic gold medal is never certain. An injury could end her career before it starts. She could decide to quit at any time, or the experts could be wrong about her supposedly brilliant future. At any rate, she's years away from being able to help her family. It could easily cost them more than $100,000 before Ritu becomes a professional. In addition, they have their two other children to consider. They will also need to pay for their college educations. ⑤

The Financial Picture: Running in the Red The Pandits spend about $600 a month more than Ray earns. They were able to make up this deficit last year by taking a loan from Ray's sister.

ANNUAL INCOME	
Ray's salary	$95,000
Loan from sister	$10,000
TOTAL	$105,000

YEARLY EXPENSES	
Ritu's ice skating	$6,000
Income taxes	7,681
Car expenses	14,400
Home mortgage	36,000
Clothing	6,000
Medical expenses	8,000
Food	7,200
Electricity/Gas	6,000
Vacations	6,000
Entertainment	4,500
Furniture and appliances	3,600
Repairs	3,000
Charity donations	2,500
Other	2,300
TOTAL	$113,181

A. Checking Your Comprehension

Answer the questions about the reading. Write the answers in your notebook.

1. Look back at your prediction on page 118. Was it correct?
2. How is Ritu Pandit different from other children her age?
3. What special expenses do the Pandits have because of Ritu?
4. What are Ritu's plans for the future?
5. What other special expenses do the Pandits have?
6. Does Ray Pandit make a good salary? Is it enough to cover all of his expenses?

B. Making Inferences

What inferences can you make about the reading? Answer the questions below.

1. Why did the Pandits decide not to send Ritu to live with another family?
2. Could Ray work any harder?
3. What kind of person do you think Ray is?
4. The reading says that Ray has no insurance. If something happened to him—if he became seriously ill or had an accident—how might this affect the different members of his family?

C. Topics for Discussion

Discuss the following questions with your classmates.

1. What is the Pandits' overall financial situation? Do you think they can afford to pay for Ritu's ice skating expenses?
2. What are some of the benefits of having a child who is so talented?
3. The article mentions the financial difficulties of having a very talented child. What other difficulties might there be?
4. Which of these sayings about money does Ray Pandit probably believe?

   • "Easy come, easy go."   "A penny saved is a penny earned."

READING STRATEGY: More Practice with Organization

Sometimes even fairly short texts have different parts. Sometimes the different parts are easy to see because the author gives each part a subtitle. However, even if there are no subtitles, it is important to recognize the different sections. One way to identify different sections is to look for a change in the general topic or focus of a reading.

Look at Reading 3. What is the topic of the first several paragraphs? Then look at the end of the reading. What is the topic there? Now, can you find where the topic changes?

1. **Reading 3 has three different parts. Two of the parts are text. What is the third part?**

2. **Complete the chart by writing on the lines the purpose of each part of Reading 3. Then, for sections I and II fill in the boxes with the paragraph topics. For section III, fill in the box with a description of the formatting used to achieve the purpose of that section.**

SECTION I

Purpose of this section: _____

SECTION II

Purpose of this section: _____

SECTION III

Purpose of this section: _____

VOCABULARY STRATEGY:
Using General Knowledge to Guess the Meaning of Unknown Words

You have already learned that you can use your general knowledge to predict the topic of readings. You can also use your general knowledge of the world to guess the meaning of unknown words.

Look at this sentence:

He drives a 1995 Lexus.

If you do not know what the word **Lexus** means, you can guess. First of all, it starts with a capital letter. What does that tell you?

Next, you can see that it is something that a person drives. What kinds of things can a person drive?

It also has a number before it. What does this number probably mean?

What do you guess a **Lexus** is?

Look at the underlined words in these sentences and use your general knowledge to guess what they mean. Write your guesses on the lines.

1. He has no <u>life insurance</u>. So, if anything happens to him, his family has no financial protection.

   _____

2. They also hired a tutor to help her with her school work because she often misses school when she goes to <u>competitions</u>.

   _____

3. Her coach here in Sweet Springs is good, but even she says that Ritu will need a world-class coach if she is going to achieve her full potential as a skater. That means sending her to live at one of the major ice-skating training <u>facilities</u>.

   _____

4. There will also be heavy travel expenses because Maribel and Ritu will go home to visit at least once a month. It is easy to see how the family's expenses could get <u>out of hand</u>.

   _____

5. It is easy to see why the family is $18,000 in debt and adding $600 a month <u>in the red</u>.

   _____

6. They were able to make up the <u>deficit</u> last year by taking a loan from Ray's sister.

   _____

Step 3: Note Useful Information

Look back at Reading 3. Which part will be the most useful for Unit Task 1? Now look at the text section and highlight or underline the most useful information for your purpose.

F. Building Your Vocabulary

Another good way to learn new words is to organize them into categories according to their meanings. Below are three categories that you could use for Reading 3.

DEBT EXPRESSIONS	MONEY VERBS	MONEY NOUNS
be in debt	pay≠earn	bills
be in the red/run in the red	borrow≠lend	payments
file for bankruptcy	buy≠sell	debts
deficit	spend≠save	consumer
(expenses) get out of hand	hire	cost
	rent	

Use some of the words and phrases above to describe the Pandit family's financial situation. Write your sentences in your notebook.

G. Writing Your Ideas

Look at the writing topics below. Choose at least one and write about it.

1. Do you know anyone who lives like the family in Reading 3? Explain their situation.

2. What is your philosophy about managing money? Are you a saver or a spender? Explain.

H. Making Connections

1. **What would Ben Franklin probably think of the Pandit family's finances? Why?**

2. **Reading 3 doesn't mention credit cards (see Reading 2), but the Pandit family has found other ways to go into debt. To whom do they owe money? Do you think this is better or worse than owing money on credit cards? Why?**

UNIT TASK 1:
Giving Financial Advice

The Pandit family has some serious financial problems. Your first task in this unit is to give them advice on their financial situation.

Your report may include suggestions for:

- ways to save money
- ways to make more money
- ways to plan for their financial future (save money)
- ways to get help with medical and education costs

You may do this task in a group, with a partner, or by yourself. For each of your suggestions, give your reasons. Try to be as realistic as possible (for example, do not suggest that the family should cut their expenses in half). Also, remember to think about cultural and social issues as well (for example, Rajiv Pandit may come from a culture where it is not usual for married women to hold jobs outside the home).

Your report should also discuss the future. You may want to show how their savings will grow over time and/or how long it will take them to get out of debt using your plan.

Your report may be written or oral.

Complete the following steps in order to help you to do Unit Task 1.

1. Analyze the Pandit family's finances and complete this table.

SUGGESTIONS FOR CUTTING EXPENSES

Type of Expense	Current Amount Spent	Suggested Amount to Spend in Future	Reason

2. Can you think of any ways that the Pandits can make more money? Write them below.

_____

_____

_____

3. Can you think of any ways that the Pandit family might receive assistance for medical or education expenses?

_____

_____

_____

4. Do you think it is realistic for the Pandit family to try to save any money? How? How important is this in their present situation? Explain.

_____

_____

_____

PART B UNIT TASK 2: EVALUATING YOUR LIFESTYLE

Identify the Information You Need

1. **Read the instructions for Unit Task 2 on page 145. Think about the information that you will need to do it. Write questions that will help you to do Unit Task 2 on the lines below. The answers to some of the questions will be different for each person.**

PERSONAL QUESTIONS

1. Do I have enough money to pay my bills _____ ?

2. _____ ?

3. _____ ?

4. _____ ?

5. _____ ?

LIFESTYLE-CHOICE QUESTIONS

6. _____ ?

7. _____ ?

8. _____ ?

9. _____ ?

10. _____ ?

2. Compare your questions with your classmates' questions. Are there any questions that you want to add to your list? Copy your final list of questions into your notebook.

3. Now look ahead to Readings 4–6. Which of them might give you the answers to each question? Draw a chart like the one on page 70, exercise 3, into your notebook. Write the question numbers and the reading numbers on the lines.

READING 4: "ENOUGH!"

Step 1: Preview the Reading

1. Where should you look first when you preview? What might this text be about?

2. Why do you think the author decided to start with a quotation? Does it give you any more information about the article?

3. Have you read or heard anything about this topic? Do you have any opinions about this topic? Why do you think people might want to earn less money? Tell your classmates.

4. Look back at the list of questions you wrote in your notebook for Unit Task 2. Which questions do you think this article may answer? Put a check mark (✓) next to them.

Step 2: Read Closely

1. Read the text. The first time you read, cover up the margin questions. Look for the answers to the questions you checked in your notebook. Write any answers that you find next to your questions.

2. Read the text again. Use the margin questions to help you.

READING 4

Enough! More and More Americans are Finding Satisfaction in Earning (and Spending) Less Money

by JIM MOTAVALLI

"The world's richest man is a poor man at times compared to the man with a satisfied mind."
—*traditional folk song*

1. What does this paragraph tell you about the text?

1 Americans are the world's greatest consumers. However, many people are beginning to realize that this materialism is slowly destroying the environment. So, some people are changing how they live. They are starting to live simpler, less wasteful lives.

2 Joe Dominguez and his partner Vicki Robin are two of the leaders of this

movement toward simplicity. They are the authors of the best-selling book *Your Money Or Your Life* and directors of the New Road Map Foundation. They offer their followers a simple message: You don't have to have a high-stress life. You can simplify your life and enjoy it more. You can stop being so wasteful and materialistic. You don't have to be a part of America's consumer culture.

3 Is there a lot of dissatisfaction with the American work-buy-spend-and-throw-away lifestyle? In a poll conducted last summer, 66 percent of the people said they would be happier if "they were able to spend more time with family and friends." Only 15 percent said that they would feel more satisfied if they "had nicer things in their homes."

4 Americans are trying to live simpler lives because they can see that our consumer culture has replaced values with material goods. Working long hours and making more money gives us more buying power than ever; however, it is not making us happy. In fact, it's making us miserable. According to the Merck poll, 82 percent of Americans agree that "most of us buy and consume far more than we need."

5 Merck's poll also found that 28 percent of Americans are actually trying to change the way that they live. They "voluntarily made changes in their [lives] that resulted in making less money" in order to have "a more balanced life." One person who did just that was Anna Quindlen. She was a journalist at the *New York Times*. Everyone expected that she would become the next editor. Therefore, they were very surprised when she quit her job to stay home with her children and write novels. Another successful person who decided that his family was more important than his career was William Galston, an advisor to President Clinton. Galston quit his job when he got a letter from his 10-year-old son, who wrote, "Baseball's no fun when there's no one there to cheer for you."

6 Galston and Quindlen are part of the 51 percent of Americans who "would rather have more free time, even if it means less money." That's not surprising when you find out that per capita consumption (the amount we spend per person) has risen 45 percent since 1970, but the quality of life has decreased 51 percent. Another survey found that approximately one third of all Americans would take a 20 percent cut in their income if they or their spouses could work fewer hours.

7 According to Dr. Juliet Schor, the Harvard economist who is the author of *The Overworked American,* in the last 20 years American workers have added one month of work per year to their

schedules. "U.S. manufacturing employees work 320 hours more a year than workers in Germany or France," says Schor. She believes that we need to change our attitude toward work and money. "Why are we choosing money over time?" she asks. "We could have our 1948 standard of living by working only half the number of hours per week that people worked in 1948."

8   The new movement toward "voluntary simplicity" is still relatively small, but it's growing rapidly. (For now, most Americans feel dissatisfied with their lives, but find it difficult to change.) It would take a powerful force to completely change America's consumerist way of thinking. Surveys show that a majority of American young people actually believe that it's "extremely important" to have at least two cars, the latest clothes, an expensive stereo and a vacation home. In 1987, a poll found that 93 percent of American teenage girls considered shopping to be their favorite activity.

10. In paragraph 9, what does the word *nevertheless* signal?

9   Nevertheless, a great change may be at work in America today. *Your Money Or Your Life* has now sold more than 400,000 copies since it was published in 1992. This, obviously, could have made Robin and Dominguez rich. However, they haven't kept any of the book's profits. All of the money has gone to their foundation. They live on $6,000 a year each.

11. In paragraph 10, can you use your general knowledge to guess the meaning of *career ladder*?

12. Which *program* is referred to in paragraph 11?

13. In paragraph 11, can you guess the meaning of *straightforward*? What clues did you use?

10   "I was working in the theater, trying to go up the career ladder," says Robin. "But then, twenty-five years ago, I met my partner, Joe Dominguez." Dominguez grew up poor but got rich working on Wall Street. He helped people make money by investing in the stock market. That job showed him that money shouldn't be so important in people's lives. "When you get rich, you get more money, but you don't necessarily get any happier," he says.

11   Dominguez created a nine-step program to teach people how to simplify their lives. "Through the program you discover how much is enough for you to have a comfortable life, with nothing in excess," Robin says. "You learn how you can save most of what you earn so that you have a nest-egg that makes money for you. It's a very, very simple, straightforward and practical process." Volunteerism is another important part of their program. First, you cut your expenses and save enough money so that you do not have to work so much. Then, you can work as a volunteer in organizations which do good work but do not have enough money to pay salaries.

12   Dominguez and Robin know that voluntary simplicity is also important on a global level. "It's becoming clear that we cannot continue to consume resources as quickly as we are," Robin says. "If other people in the world imitate the American way of trying to buy happiness, we will destroy our world. What other people should see is that even though we're the richest nation on Earth, many people are not happy. Studies show we're no happier now than we were in 1957, before there were microwaves in every kitchen and computers in every bedroom. We've hit a happiness ceiling."

A. Checking Your Comprehension

1. Answer the questions about the readings on the lines below.

1. What is Joe Dominguez's and Vicki Robin's philosophy called?

   _____

2. Are Americans working more or less than they were twenty years ago?

   _____

3. The reading describes a problem and gives a solution. What are they?

   _____

2. Look at the text and complete each statement with the correct percentage. An example has been done for you.

1. _66_ % of Americans would like to have more free time at home.

2. ____ % of Americans would like to have nicer things.

3. ____ % of Americans think that most people buy more things than they need.

4. Americans spend ____% more now than they did in 1970.

5. ____ % of Americans are trying to simplify their lives.

6. ____ % of Americans would be willing to have less money if they could work fewer hours.

7. More than ____ % of young people in America think that cars, clothes, and stereos are very important.

8. ____ % of American teenage girls shop for fun.

B. Making Inferences

What inferences can you make about the reading? Answer the questions below.

1. Does the author agree with or criticize the simplicity movement? Why do you think so?

2. What do you think is the purpose of the New Road Map Foundation? Why is it called that?

3. Does the author believe that most Americans are likely to change their lifestyles very soon? Why or why not?

4. What is the connection between the simplicity movement and environmentalism?

C. Topics for Discussion

Discuss the following questions with your classmates.

1. How does the quotation at the beginning of the reading relate to the text? Do you agree with the quotation?

2. Some people believe that consumerism is necessary for the United States to be strong. Why do you think that they believe this? Do you believe it?

3. Joe Dominguez is worried about consumerism spreading to other countries. Is consumerism a problem in your native country? Why or why not?

4. Do you think that having fewer things and less money will make more people happier? Why or why not?

D. Strategies for Unknown Vocabulary

VOCABULARY STRATEGY:
Understanding the Meaning of Suffixes

Suffixes often change the part of speech of words. In addition, suffixes have their own meaning or use. It may be difficult to learn the meanings of all of the suffixes, but it is helpful to learn the meanings of the most common ones.

Look at these suffixes. What is their meaning or use?

		MEANING OR USE
Paris	Paris<u>ian</u>	_____
Brazil	Brazil<u>ian</u>	_____
Canada	Canad<u>ian</u>	_____

Example: Parisians are people who live in **Paris.**

organize	organiza<u>tion</u>	_____
educate	educa<u>tion</u>	_____
explore	explora<u>tion</u>	_____

Example: Columbus **explored** the Caribbean. His **explorations** took many years.

| piano | pian<u>ist</u> | _____ |
| commune | commun<u>ist</u> | _____ |

Example: My sister learned to play the **piano** when she was four. She is an excellent **pianist.**

Look at Reading 4. How many words can you find that have these suffixes?

Now turn the page and answer the questions.

1. **Look at the words below and try to guess the meaning of the suffix *-ism*. Remember that suffixes can also change the part of speech. What part of speech is a word that ends in *-ism*? Write your answers on the lines below.**

   1. commune

      Commun**ism**

      A **commune** is a place where a group of people lives together and share their money and property.

      Communism is political system in which the government owns all of the businesses and property and uses it for the good of the people.

   2. consumer

      consumer**ism**

      The United States is a country of **consumers.**

      Consumerism is ruining the country.

   3. material

      material**ism**

      He is rich in friends and family although he doesn't own a lot of **material** goods.

      Materialism and consumerism go hand in hand.

   4. volunteer

      volunteer**ism**

      We need **volunteers** to help collect food and clothing.

      The idea of **volunteerism** is getting more popular today.

   Meaning of the suffix *-ism*: _____

   Part of speech of words ending in *-ism*: _____

2. **Can you think of any other words that end in *-ism*? Do they also fit your definition of *-ism*?**

Even if you do not know the meaning of a suffix or a prefix, you can often guess the meaning of new words by relating them to words that you know. It is also helpful if you can figure out the part of speech of the words that you do not know.

Look at the underlined words. How are they related? Write the part of speech for each word on the line.

	Part of Speech
The problem isn't <u>simple</u>.	_____
Americans are trying to <u>simplify</u> their lives.	_____
The voluntary <u>simplicity</u> movement is growing.	_____
They are starting to live <u>simpler</u>, less wasteful lives.	_____

3. **Look at Reading 4 to find all of the words related to each of the words below. Write the words and the part of speech of each word that you find on the lines.**

   1. volunteer _____

   2. consumer _____

   3 satisfy _____

   4. material _____

   5. waste _____

Step 3: Note Useful Information

1. **Look at Unit Task 2 on page 145 again. Are there any new ideas or information in the reading that may help you to do this task?**

2. **Draw a vertical line (|) in the right margin to mark the new ideas that you find. How many ideas you mark and which ideas you mark will depend on your present lifestyle and whether you are interested in changing it.**

E. Writing Your Ideas

Look at the writing topics below. Choose at least one and write about it.

   1. Are you satisfied with your life? What do you think would make your life better—more money to spend or more free time? Explain.

   2. If you have a job, think of a way (or ways) in which changing it might make your life easier or happier. Would it be possible to make this change? Why or why not? Explain.

F. Building Your Vocabulary

Use these steps to build your vocabulary with words from the reading.

1. Look at the "money management" word web you made in your notebook. Now start a "lifestyle" word web. Use words about lifestyles that you already know. Then look at Reading 4 for more words to add to the word web.

2. Make a separate list of words from Reading 4 that you think will be generally useful.

3. Use each new word in a sentence and write the sentences in your notebook.

G. Making Connections

1. **Think about the family that you read about in Reading 3 (the Pandits). What concept in Reading 4 do they illustrate? Do you think it might be possible for them to change their lives, as suggested in Reading 4?**

2. **What concepts from Reading 1 are important to Joe Dominguez's philosophy? Explain.**

READING 5: "CHANGING YOUR LIFESTYLE"

Step 1: Preview the Reading

1. **Where do you think this reading is from? Who wrote it? What connection do you think it has with Reading 4?**

2. **This column has two parts. What are they?**

3. **Skim the text to find out which of the following is probably the most important kind of information given in this reading.**
   a. some ideas on how to you can start saving money today
   b. an example of a family that was able to save a lot of money
   c. more reasons why Americans should live simpler lives

4. **Scan the list at the end of the text to find this information:**
   a. What percentage of Americans lived in air-conditioned homes in 1987?
   b. How much did American advertisers spend per person in 1950?

5. **Look back at the list of questions you wrote in your notebook for Unit Task 2. Which questions do you think this article may answer? Put a check mark (✓) next to them.**

1. **Read the text. The first time you read, cover up the margin questions. Look for the answers to the questions you checked in your notebook. Write any answers that you find next to your questions.**

2. **Read the text again. Use the margin questions to help you.**

READING 5

Changing Your Lifestyle

by JIM MOTAVALLI

Amy has sometimes visited as many as 30 yard and garage sales a day looking for bargains.

1   When the voluntary simplicity movement first started, the idea of "retiring" from the consumer culture was more ideal than real. Buying and spending was, after all, supposed to be a lifetime commitment. But now the movement has developed and some people have learned that they can actually escape from consumerism.

2   Amy Dacyczyn (pronounced like "decision") is an excellent example. She's the editor of the Maine-based *Tightwad Gazette,* a monthly newsletter that serves as a practical guide to cutting down expenses and living a simpler life. (Since the *Gazette* first came out, it has gotten competition from many others such as the *Cheapskate Monthly, Living Cheap News, Penny Pincher Times, The Frugal Bugle, The SAVing Source, Saving Green* and *Downscaling for Professionals.)*

3   Dacyczyn says she started the newsletter after she and her husband, a retired military officer, saved $49,000 in seven years on a combined yearly income of $30,000. "I thought that what we had done was something most people didn't believe possible," she says. They saved the money by being frugal. For example, they rarely bought things new. Amy has sometimes visited as many as 30 yard sales a day looking for bargains. In addition they let their six kids choose one — and only one — new Christmas present. Dacyczyn says that "most people just aren't really being honest with themselves about money. They believe the mythology they get from television." If people are serious about changing their lives, Dacyczyn says, they should "pay attention to

Margin questions:

1. What is Dacyczyn an example of?

2. Look at the names in paragraph 2. Are they necessary for you to understand the article?

3. Can you guess the meaning of the word *frugal* in paragraph 3?

4. In paragraph 3, are there enough clues to guess the meaning of *mythology*? If not, do you need to look it up?

5. What are *disposables?*

6. Can you guess the general meaning of *penny-pinching?*

7. Can you use general knowledge to guess the meaning of a *six-figure income?*

the disposables, like food, entertainment and clothing. The areas where people really waste the most are where they should make big changes immediately."

4 All that penny-pinching was successful. Dacyczyn's very profitable newsletter has a circulation of 45,000. Its profits are combined with the income she gets from writing books and her husband's retirement money. That means this very frugal family has a six-figure income. That's more than enough to live comfortably. However, they still buy most of their clothes, toys and household items second-hand.

5 Dacyczyn says that she has received many offers to write newspaper columns, host television shows and write more books. But, frankly she's not interested. In fact, she's closing the newsletter this year because she thinks it has said everything it needed to say. "The old issues and the books are out there," she says, "and there's just not much more I could add to them."

6 In retirement, Dacyczyn, who's only 40, plans to refinish furniture, make quilts, read novels, research her family history and become a volunteer, too. "I don't think I'll have trouble finding things to do," she says.

CONSUMPTION INDEX

U.S. advertising costs per person (in dollars)	in 1950: in 1989:	198 498
Percent of retail sales which take place in shopping centers	in the United States: in Spain:	55 4
Percent of Americans with air-conditioning	in 1960: in 1987:	15 64
Average number of hours working Americans spend driving per week:		9
Percent of new cars that are air-conditioned:		90
Steel consumption per person	in the U.S.: in Bangladesh:	417 5
Percent of Chinese owning color televisions:	in 1982: in 1987:	1 35
Percent of world population living in industrialized countries:		20
Percent of the world's timber and energy consumed by that 20 percent:		75
Percent of the world's radioactive wastes and chloroflurocarbons made by that 20 percent:		90
U.S. world ranking as producer of municipal waste per person:		1
U.S. world ranking as producer of greenhouse gas emissions:		1

SOURCES: Center for the Study of Commercialism; Technology Review; The Harwood Group; U.S. News and World Report; President's Council on Sustainable Development.

A. Checking Your Comprehension

1. Complete this chart about the person described in the article.

Name _____ Age _____

Occupation _____

Marital Status: ☐ married ☐ divorced ☐ widowed ☐ single

Children _____

Future Plans _____

Philosophy of Life _____

2. Look at the consumption index on page 136. Find the statistics that support each of these statements and write them on the lines below.

1. People in the United States consume more than people in many other countries.

   _____

2. Consumerism is growing around the world.

   _____

3. The majority of the world's resources are used by a minority of the world's population.

   _____

4. Some things which used to be luxuries are now considered necessities.

   _____

5. The United States is one of the world's greatest polluting nations.

   _____

B. Making Inferences

What inferences can you make about the reading? Answer the questions below.

1. What kind of person do you think Amy Dacyczyn is? What makes you think this?

2. Do you think it is difficult to save $49,000 in seven years when you have an income of $30,000? Why?

3. What do you think is the "mythology" people get from television?

4. What can we infer from the figures in the consumption index about consumerism in America? How does it compare to consumerism in other countries?

C. Topics for Discussion

Discuss the following questions with your classmates.

1. Would you like to be one of Amy Dacyczyn's children? Why or why not?

2. If you were Amy Dacyczyn, would you stop publishing the newsletter? Why or why not?

3. Do you think that Amy Dacyczyn is rich or poor? Why?

D. Reading Strategies

READING STRATEGY:
More Practice Recognizing Important Ideas and Details

In Reading 3, you practiced deciding which ideas were important and which were details. Important ideas are closely related to paragraph topics because the important ideas in a text are generally about the topic of a paragraph.

Look at the diagram. Fill in the boxes with the topic of each paragraph in Reading 5. If there is more than one line in the box, add details from the paragraph, too.

VOCABULARY STRATEGY: More Practice with Suffixes

Suffixes often change the part of speech of a root word, as in the example below:

accept + able → acceptable

Accept is a verb, but when the suffix **-able** is added, the resulting word is an adjective. Look at more examples of this in the table below. Copy the table into your notebook and complete it.

root	part of speech	new word	part of speech	meaning of suffix
accept		acceptable		
live		livable		
reason		reasonable		
fashion		fashionable		

1. Answer these questions about the table you completed.

1. Look at the root words that can combine with the suffix **-able**. What parts of speech are they? _____   _____

2. Now look at the new words that were created with the suffix **-able**. What part of speech are they? _____

   (The root words which combine with a particular suffix are often all the same part of speech, but they do not have to be. However, the new words that are formed (root word + suffix) are almost always the same part of speech.)

3. There are three words in Reading 5 (including the chart) which contain **-able**. What are they? What part of speech are they?

   _____   _____   _____

2. One of the words in Reading 5 has the suffix -*able* and another suffix. What is the second suffix? What is its function?

   _____

Step 3: Note Useful Information

Are there a lot of facts that are useful for Unit Task 2 in this reading? If not, are there any specific ideas that might help you to do Unit Task 2? What are they? Write them in your notebook.

F. Building Your Vocabulary

Use these steps to build your vocabulary with words from the reading.

1. The names of the newsletters given in paragraph 2 of Reading 5 contain several words which can be used to describe people who are careful with their money. Look at the titles. Can you figure out which words these are? Write them on the lines below.

   _____   _____   _____

2. Look up the words above in a dictionary. Are they positive words or negative words? Add them to the word web on "lifestyles" in your notebook.

3. In your notebook, make a separate list of words from Reading 5 that you think will be generally useful. Use each new word in a sentence and write the sentences in your notebook.

G. Writing Your Ideas

Look at the writing topics below. Choose at least one and write about it.

1. Do you ever waste money? What do you waste it on?

2. Would you like to live like Amy Dacyczyn? Explain.

3. Do you know some ways that people can save money? Explain.

H. Making Connections

1. **How are the lifestyles of the Pandit family and the Dacyczyn family different? Are there any ways that they are the same? Which household would you rather live in?**

2. **Compare the financial situation of the Pandit and the Dacyczyn families. One family has $105,000 in income and $18,000 in debts, and the other one has $30,000 in income and $49,000 in savings over seven years. How is this possible?**

3. **Would Joe Dominguez (Reading 4) approve of the Dacyczyn's lifestyle? Why or why not?**

Step 1: Preview the Reading

1. Where should you look first when previewing this reading? What do you think the topic of this reading is?

2. Now read the first and last paragraphs. Stop reading if you think the paragraph will not help you to find out more about the topic.

3. Were both paragraphs helpful? Why or why not?

4. What do you think the main idea of the reading is?

5. Look back at the list of questions you wrote in your notebook for Unit Task 2. Which questions do you think this article may answer? Put a check mark (✓) next to them.

Step 2: Read Closely

1. Read the text. The first time you read, cover up the margin questions. Look for the answers to the questions you checked in your notebook. Write any answers that you find next to your questions.

2. Read the text again. Use the margin questions to help you.

READING 6

1. Does this paragraph give you an overview of the text? If not, where is the main idea introduced?

Together In Giving

Volunteering gives children a sense of community responsibility—and brings the family closer together

BY MARILYN GARDNER

In some cases, entire families are volunteering together.

1   When Rebecca Spaide started planning her ninth birthday party, her mother, Deborah, gave her an unusual idea. She suggested that instead of guests buying gifts for Rebecca, they could bring presents for people who were living in a local homeless shelter. Rebecca agreed. When 16 friends arrived for her recent party, they brought all kinds of things—including food, towels and blankets. The next day, Spaide drove Rebecca and four friends to the shelter to deliver her birthday presents. "It felt good," Rebecca said. "I'm giving something to them instead of to me, because I have so much and they have so little."

2   Rebecca's feelings are not unusual. Volunteerism is growing across the

2. Which two sentences give you the main idea of paragraph 2? Find information in paragraphs 3–11 that develops this idea.

3. What is the purpose of paragraph 8?

4. In paragraph 9, can you guess the general meaning of *outgoing*? Is it a positive or negative quality?

5. In paragraph 10, what may help you to guess the meaning of *abstract*?

6. Can you use your general knowledge to guess the meaning of *soup kitchen* in paragraph 11?

United States today. In fact, in some cases entire families are volunteering together. Parents are finding that they can teach their children about community responsibility by including them in their volunteer efforts. Another added benefit is that families get to spend more time together.

3   "It's a wonderful experience to share something as fulfilling as helping meet another person's needs with other members of your family," Spaide said. "How better could parents teach their kids values?"

4   Sheryl Nefstead, an associate professor at the University of Minnesota in St. Paul says, "People are trying to put more emphasis on family togetherness, and they're looking for ways to help young people have a feeling of hope and satisfaction." Volunteerism is also growing because people have a greater awareness of social problems and a realization that government support for the poor is decreasing.

5   In a Gallup poll done last year, more than a third of American households said volunteering together is part of family life. The most common activities include helping older people or working with youth, church or religious programs. Nearly half of volunteer families work in sports or school programs. A third are involved in environmental programs and a quarter help the homeless.

6   The Spaides have five children between the ages of 7 and 18. They have all taken part in a number of different volunteer activities such as making repairs to a public housing apartment, preparing food for the homeless and doing garden work for elderly people in their town.

7   Charity, Deborah Spaide explained, helps children and teenagers discover talents, develop skills and learn about cooperation and problem-solving. It also teaches what she calls anti-materialism. They learn that one of the best things that you can do for yourself is to do something for others.

8   For Randy Dostal of Silver Lake, Minnesota, family volunteering takes two forms. At work he encourages employees to include their families in his company's volunteer activities. As a parent, he also considers volunteering an important family activity. He and his wife and their six children, who range in age from 7 to 17, spend many hours each week in church, school and community activities. "I was always brought up on volunteerism," Dostal said. "My parents did it, so it seems like the natural thing to do. If I can give something back or do something for someone, it makes me feel good all over."

9   Dostal also sees other benefits in family volunteering. "It's made our children more outgoing," he said. "They're able to work with anyone, no matter what race or nationality. They're willing to do things without anyone having to pressure them. They don't say 'no' very often. As they go on to college and then get jobs, volunteering is going to make a big difference in their lives."

10   Spaide emphasizes the importance of giving children volunteer projects that allow them to see results quickly. Calling this "hands-on charity," she offered the example of "making a sandwich and handing it to someone who's hungry." Least effective for children, she said, is "abstract charity." She explained, "It's not meaningful for children to just give someone their money without understanding how it's going to help."

11   For families interested in volunteering, Spaide suggests calling soup kitchens, homeless shelters and nursing homes to ask what they need. Volunteer programs run by businesses, youth groups and churches also offer possibilities for service.

12   Summing up three advantages of family volunteering, Dostal said, "It obviously benefits the community that's served. It benefits the family for serving together. And it benefits each individual in the family. How can you lose?"   □

A. Checking Your Comprehension

1. According to Reading 6, all of these people think that volunteerism is important. What did each of them say or do to show that that is true? Write the answers in your notebook.

   Rebecca Spaide   Deborah Spaide

   Sheryl Nefstead   Randy Dostal

2. What are some examples of volunteer activities that are mentioned in the text? Write them in your notebook.

3. Complete the chart below with information from the text.

   BENEFITS OF VOLUNTEERING

   to the community _____

   to children _____

   to adults _____

   to the family _____

   to other groups in the community _____

   _____

B. Making Inferences

What inferences can you make about the reading? Answer the questions below.

1. Why did Rebecca Spaide's mother suggest that Rebecca and her friends give presents to people in the homeless shelter?

2. What are some of the "values" the parents in this reading want their children to learn?

3. Why is "hands-on" charity better for children than "abstract" charity?

C. Topics for Discussion

Discuss the following questions with your classmates.

1. Can you think of any other benefits of volunteering that are not mentioned in the reading?

2. Have you ever volunteered to help a community organization? What did you do?

3. How is volunteering viewed in your community or country? Can you give some specific examples?

READING STRATEGY: More Practice with Guiding Sentences

"Guiding sentences" help you predict what information is coming when you read. When you have a good idea what the author is going to tell you next, you will understand it more easily.

Look at the sentence below. What do the underlined words tell you about information to come?

For Randy Dostal of Silver Lake, Minn., family volunteering takes <u>two forms</u>.

Look at these sentences. Which words help you predict the information that will follow? Underline them.

1. Dostal also sees other benefits in family volunteering.

2. Summing up three advantages of family volunteering, Dostal said...

3. Another added benefit is...

E. Strategies for Unknown Vocabulary

VOCABULARY STRATEGY: More Practice with Suffixes

Here are two more common suffixes. Can you guess their meanings? Write them on the lines.

use**ful** _____

success**ful**

hope**ful**

care**ful**

child**less** _____

hope**less**

care**less**

---

1. **Can you find an example of each of these suffixes in Reading 6? What kind of reading will you need to do in order to find them? Can you think of any other words that end with *-ful* or *-less*?**

2. **Make a list of suffixes and their meanings in your notebook.**

What does this reading have to say about lifestyle choices? Are any of the ideas useful for Unit Task 2?

F. Building Your Vocabulary

Use these steps to build your vocabulary with words from the reading.

1. Look at Reading 6. Can you find any words about volunteering? Add them to the "lifestyle" word web in your notebook.
2. In your notebook, make a separate list of words from Reading 5 that you think will be generally useful.
3. Use each new word in a sentence and write the sentences in your notebook.

G. Writing Your Ideas

Look at the writing topics below. Choose at least one and write about it.

1. Have you or your family ever received help from people in your community? How did it make you feel? Explain.
2. Who takes the responsibility to help needy people in your community or country? Why? Explain.

H. Making Connections

What concept can you find repeated in Readings 4–6? What concept is found in Readings 4 and 5 but not in Reading 6 ?

Unit Task 2:
Evaluating Your Lifestyle

In Readings 4–6, you read about people who are cutting their expenses by deciding what is important in their lives and changing their lifestyles. Your second task in this unit is to evaluate your own lifestyle and, if you decide it is necessary, make a plan for change.

You should look at the following aspects of your life:

- the way that you manage money (You do not need to talk about amounts of money here. Discuss how you feel about money and what you do about it.)
- your attitudes about the importance of material goods
- your attitudes about the importance of work, friends, and family
- your attitude about community involvement

This task asks you to think about your own lifestyle and to decide if you like it or want to change it. Because of this, it will probably be easier to do this report alone. You do not have to change your lifestyle according to any of the philosophies presented in this unit. You only need to think about the questions raised in the readings. You may decide that you are quite satisfied with some or all of these aspects in your life.

This Unit Task should be a written report.

Complete the following steps to help you do Unit Task 2:

1. Are you satisfied with your lifestyle? Why or why not?

   _____

   _____

   _____

   _____

2. Is your financial situation as good as you would like it? If not, which areas would you like to change? What ideas do you have for changing them? (Some people consider their financial situation very private. Only give as much information as you feel comfortable giving here.)

   _____

   _____

   _____

   _____

3. Do you feel that you have enough time to do the things you really want to do in your life? If not, what would you like to change? What ideas do you have for making these changes?

   _____

   _____

   _____

   _____

4. If you feel that your life is happy, explain why you are satisfied with it. If possible, give specific examples.

   _____

   _____

   _____

   _____

5. Use ideas from Readings 1–6 to focus on the points listed in the Unit Task box on page 145 and plan your report. Your report should contain these sections:

   Material Wealth
   money management
   consumerism

   Non-material Wealth
   personal relationships
   volunteerism

Applying Your Knowledge

1. Conduct a survey about people's attitudes toward money and lifestyle. In pairs or small groups, make a list of questions to ask. You may be able to get some ideas for questions from the polls mentioned in the readings in this unit.

2. In groups, think of a volunteer activity that you could do together. It can be for an individual, your school, or your community. Do the activity and report to the class.

3. Invite a speaker from a consumer credit counseling service to talk to your class about the dangers of credit card debt.

The Electronic Link

Here are some Web sites related to money:

The Frugal Corner
http://www.frugalcorner.com/

The Pierce Study on Voluntary Simplicity
http://www.mbay.net/~pierce/index.htm

Center for the New American Dream
http://www.newdream.org/

If you cannot locate these Web sites or you would like more information, do an Internet search, using the words *volunteerism, voluntary simplicity, savings, debt,* or *credit.*

What sites did you find? Compare your answers with those of your classmates.

Now choose one Web site and fill in the information requested below. Try to find a site that gives information you can use in your Unit Task.

Name of site:_____

URL (Web address): _____

Center for the Study of Commercialism
1875 Connecticut Avenue NW Suite 300
Washington, DC 20009-5728
(202) 332-9110

Merck Family Fund
6930 Carroll Avenue, Suite 500
Takoma Park, MD 20912
(301) 270-2970

The New Road Map Foundation
P.O. Box 15981
Seattle, WA 98115
(206) 527-0437

The PEN Exchange
c/o McGee Street Foundation
P.O. Box 56756
Washington, DC 20040
(301) 608-8008

Teaching Your Kids to Care: How to Discover and Develop the Spirit of Charity in Your Children. Rebecca Spaide. Secaucus, NJ: Carol Publishing Group, 1995.

Your Money or Your Life: Transforming Your Relationship with Money and Achieving Financial Independence. Joe Dominguez and Vickie Robin. New York: Penguin, 1993.

📖 **See the Additional Readings for this unit on pages 212–213.**

Essay Questions

Choose one of the topics below and write an essay on it.

1. Do you think the suggestions in this unit about volunteerism or simplicity are useful or relevant for your community or culture? Why or why not? Explain.

2. What is one specific area of your life that you would like to simplify? Why? What would you need to do in order to simplify it?

3. Many people believe that their lives would be better if they just had a little more money. How would your lifestyle change if your salary increased by 30%?

4. If your employer offered you $10,000 more per year for ten more hours of work each week (or two hours more per day), would you accept the offer? Why or why not? Explain.

5. If your employer offered you a chance to work two fewer hours each day for 25% less salary, would you accept it? Why or why not? Explain.

Evaluating Your Progress

Think about the skills and strategies that you used in this unit. Check (✓) the correct boxes.

	NEVER	SOMETIMES	OFTEN	ALWAYS
1. I was able to predict the information that I would find in a reading.	☐	☐	☐	☐
2. When I previewed, I thought about where a reading came from and what I knew about the topic.	☐	☐	☐	☐
3. I was able to predict the purpose of a reading.	☐	☐	☐	☐
4. I was able to recognize which ideas were important and which were details.	☐	☐	☐	☐
5. I was able to find the main ideas of paragraphs.	☐	☐	☐	☐
6. I looked up words in the dictionary only when absolutely necessary.	☐	☐	☐	☐
7. When I looked up a word in the dictionary, I was able to find the correct meaning.	☐	☐	☐	☐
8. I was able to use general knowledge to guess the meanings of unknown words.	☐	☐	☐	☐
9. I was able to find relationships between words in order to help guess their meanings.	☐	☐	☐	☐
10. I thought about parts of speech when I was trying to figure out the meaning of unknown words.	☐	☐	☐	☐

Setting Your Reading Goals

1. Choose three items from the list above that you would like to improve. Write them below.

Goal #1 _____

Goal #2 _____

Goal #3 _____

2. Now look back at your reading goals from Unit 2 on page 96. Are you moving toward these goals?

Steven Hawking

Mozart

Kristi Yamaguchi

Jane Austen

*I*N THIS UNIT

Reading Strategies

- Learning how to read a textbook
- Understanding how examples support important ideas
- Recognizing important ideas

Strategies for Unknown Vocabulary

- Using a dictionary and a glossary
- Choosing the best dictionary definition
- Understanding complex noun phrases
- Using a vocabulary decision tree

What Kind of Smart are You?

Think About It

What do you think intelligence is? Think of someone who you think is intelligent. What qualities of that person make him or her intelligent? Look at the pictures of the people on page 150. Would you call them all intelligent? Are they all intelligent in the same way?

Looking Ahead in Unit Four

Look at each of the readings in the unit. Match the readings in the unit with the types of readings listed below. Write the reading numbers on the lines. How do you know which kind of reading each one is? (Some types of readings appear more than once in this unit.)

READING NUMBER(S)

1. an interview   _____

2. a part of a textbook _____

3. a class handout   _____

4. a magazine article   _____

Looking at the Unit Tasks

This unit has two tasks. The first one occurs after Reading 3 on page 173. You will do the second one after Reading 6 on page 198. Look for the two Unit Tasks and write their titles below.

Unit Task 1 _____

Unit Task 2 _____

Identify the Information You Need

1. **Read the instructions for Unit Task 1 on page 173. Think about the information that you will need to do it. You will probably need three different kinds of information. Two of them will be about different researchers' theories on intelligence and learning. The third kind of information will come from your own experience. Write questions on the lines below that will help you to do Unit Task 1.**

QUESTIONS ABOUT INTELLIGENCE

1. _____?
2. _____?
3. _____?
4. _____?
5. _____?

QUESTIONS ABOUT LEARNING STYLES

6. _____?
7. _____?
8. _____?
9. _____?
10. _____?

2. **Compare your questions with your classmates' questions. Are there any questions that you want to add to your list? Copy your final list of questions into your notebook.**

3. **Now look ahead to Readings 1–3. Which of them might give you the answers to each question? Draw a chart like the one on page 70, exercise 3, into your notebook. Write the question numbers and the reading numbers on the lines.**

Step 1: Preview the Reading

PREVIEWING STRATEGY:
Understanding and Using a Textbook's Format

Textbooks are usually written and organized in a way that the author feels will make them most useful for students. In order to make the best use of your textbook, it is important to find out what kinds of information the textbook contains and how it is organized before you begin to read.

Some common kinds of information that textbooks may have are

> a table of contents which contains detailed information on the content of each unit
>
> an index of important words or concepts
>
> an overview which begins each unit
>
> a unit summary
>
> lists of key terms in the unit overview or summary
>
> subtitles
>
> key words in bold type
>
> a glossary
>
> review or study questions
>
> a list of unit objectives

Which of these features will help to preview a reading or a unit? Circle them in the list above.

Which of these features can you find in this textbook? Check (✓) them in the list above.

---

1. **Reading 1 is taken from a educational psychology textbook. Look at it quickly. Which of the items from the box above can you find?**

2. **Look at the list titled "Important Terms: Lesson 1" in this reading. Now scan the reading to find the terms that are discussed in Lesson 1A. (Note: The terms not discussed in this reading will appear in Readings 5 and 6 of this unit.)**

3. **Look back at the list of questions you wrote in your notebook for Unit Task 1. Which questions do you think this reading will answer? Put a check mark (✓) next to them.**

1. **Read the text. The first time you read, cover up the margin questions. Look for the answers to the questions you checked in your notebook. Write any answers that you find next to your questions.**

2. **Read the text again. Use the margin questions to help you.**

READING 1

INTRODUCTION TO INTELLIGENCE

OVERVIEW: LESSON 1

1. What does this paragraph tell you about what came before in the textbook?

In this lesson we will discuss some of the difficulties faced when trying to define intelligence (IQ) and measure it in children and adults. The nature/nurture[1] issue comes up again with this lesson. In recent years, researchers have focused on the ways that environment influences intelligence. We will also discuss schooling, including what makes a good school or learning environment, how teacher feedback affects students, and how helplessness is learned.

OBJECTIVES: LESSON 1

After completing this lesson you will be able to

2. How can you use this kind of information to help you as you read?

- discuss the difficulties of measuring intelligence in standardized ways

- list the characteristics that make schools more effective and compare traditional and open classrooms

- explain how teachers' prejudices can affect students' performance

IMPORTANT TERMS: LESSON 1

intelligence	open classroom
IQ test	traditional classroom
Binet	learned helplessness
mental age	mastery orientation

---

[1] "Nature/nurture" refers to the argument about whether most of a person's personality and intelligence is determined by his genes (nature) or his environment (nurture).

LESSON 1A

What Is Intelligence?

3. Do people generally agree about what intelligence is?

1 Swiss psychologist Jean Piaget would have described intelligence as the thinking ability that helps a person solve problems and adapt to his or her environment. But this definition does not include many other abilities and qualities that most of us would use to describe intelligence. Intelligence could also mean the ability to do abstract thinking, to carry out our plans, or to think logically; it also might mean everything that a person has learned in his or her lifetime.

4. What does *in other words* signal here?

2 Before 1960, some people believed that, for the most part, intelligence was innate or inborn. In other words, either you were born smart or you weren't and nothing could change that. More recently, scientists have begun to look at how a person's environment might influence the development of intelligence.

5. What is the first issue in understanding intelligence?

3 The other main issue in understanding intelligence is how to measure it. Two of the main abilities that have been measured in IQ (intelligence quotient) tests are verbal comprehension (understanding words) and the ability to think with and about numbers. IQ tests also measure other parts of intelligence such as general thinking ability, vocabulary, memory, and spatial ability[2]. However, other abilities often connected with intelligence, such as creativity, artistic and musical talent, social skills, and regular common sense, are often not included on standard IQ tests.

Testing IQ

6. What is the main idea of paragraphs 4 and 5?

4 The IQ test was designed to measure success in school. Alfred Binet was asked to develop the first IQ test in order to identify "dull" children—the children who needed additional or remedial help in school. This is important because many people might not think that school success is the only kind of intelligence, yet this is all that IQ tests measure.

7. What is a *norm?* Does the context help you understand its meaning?

5 Binet designed the test with increasing levels of difficulty so that children of different ages could pass different parts of the test. He tested many, many children, and then decided on age norms for the questions he wrote. For example, a question that most six-year-olds could answer but most five-year-olds could not answer was thought to show the average mental performance of a six-year-old.

---

[2] "Spatial ability" refers to the ability to figure out things in space. For example, someone who is good with maps and directions probably has a lot of spatial ability.

8. What is the purpose of paragraph 6?

6 The product of Binet's test was a number showing a child's mental age (MA). Mental age is changed to an IQ score by dividing the MA by the child's actual age and multiplying the result by 100. Therefore, a 6-year-old who scored at a mental age of 6 would have an IQ of 100 (6/6 x 100 = 100). This system allows us to compare the IQs of children of different ages. A 6-year-old with an MA of 3 has an IQ of 50, and a 10-year-old with an MA of 5 also has an IQ of 50. An average IQ is considered to be 100, with a standard deviation of 15 points (thus, the range of average IQs is from 85 to 115). Binet's original test was later modified by a researcher from Stanford University in California. The result is the IQ test used today, called the Stanford-Binet.

9. How does paragraph 7 connect paragraphs 4–6 with 8–11?

7 Because they were developed to predict future school success, IQ tests compare fairly well with actual school performance. What else do they predict? If we think of them as measures of intelligence, we might expect them to predict other things, such as job performance, or life satisfaction. Each of these factors has been studied in relation to IQ scores.

8 Researchers have found that the average IQ of people who have more prestigious jobs (such as doctor or lawyer) is higher than the average IQ of people in jobs with less prestige (such as farmhand or factory worker). In addition, researchers found that although there are high-IQ people in lower-prestige jobs, there are no people with low IQs in high-prestige jobs.

9 In many cases, IQ is not a good predictor of job performance. In professions with intermediate status (such as electrician), IQ made a difference in job performance. However, at the upper and lower ends, a person's IQ score did not show any relationship to success on the job.

10 Another question is whether high-IQ people are happier, healthier, or more satisfied with their lives than people with lower IQs. Terman did a study of children with very high IQs (140 or higher). He found that they generally develop a little faster. In addition, they were seen as more competent and better adjusted than children with lower IQs.

10. What does *however* signal here? What kind of information will come next?

11 However, there was a problem with his study. Terman did not choose his subjects carefully enough. His group of high-IQ students contained too many children of educated, wealthy and powerful parents. Therefore, these children had more educational opportunities, higher social standing, and more money than many of the lower-IQ children. All of these factors have been shown to correlate with high IQ. Therefore, the success of these children may have been more influenced by their social status than by their measured IQ.

(To continue reading on this topic, see Readings 5 and 6.)

A. Checking Your Comprehension

1. Look back at the explanation of IQ scores. Then calculate the IQs for these people and circle if they are high, low or average.

1. age 12   mental age 8   IQ = ____   high/low/average

2. age 14   mental age 16   IQ = ____   high/low/average

3. age 10   mental age 16   IQ = ____   high/low/average

2. Circle the word that correctly begins each sentence.

1. All/Most/Some/No   people with high IQs do well in school.

2. All/Most/Some/No   people in high prestige jobs have above-average IQs.

3. All/Most/Some/No   people in low prestige jobs have high IQs.

4. All/Most/Some/No   people in high prestige jobs have low IQs.

B. Making Inferences

What inferences can you make about the reading? Answer the questions below.

1. Do you think that the writer is in favor of IQ testing? Why or why not?

2. Does the writer believe that people with high IQs are more successful than people with average IQs?

3. Does the writer believe that intelligence is more than just the abilities a person is born with?

4. Does the writer think information about a person's IQ is useful for many purposes, or not very useful?

C. Topics for Discussion

Discuss the following questions with your classmates.

1. Have you ever taken an IQ test? If so, what was it like?

2. What are some benefits of IQ testing? What are some weaknesses?

3. If you had a child, would you have his or her IQ tested? Why or why not?

4. Do you know anyone with a high IQ? In what ways has their intelligence helped them? In what ways has it hurt them?

5. Are there other tests that are used in your country to measure intelligence?

D. Reading Strategies

READING STRATEGY: Learning How to Read a Textbook

When you read a textbook, it is helpful to use all of the different kinds of formatting and organization. They will help you to read better and more efficiently. Even when you read an ordinary text, you often have to figure out the organization. However, in a textbook the titles and subtitles often help to make the organization of the information very clear.

What are the subtitles in Reading 1?

Which other items in the list on page 153 will help you as you are reading texts closely? How can they help? Write your answer on the lines.

_____

_____

E. Strategies for Unknown Vocabulary

VOCABULARY STRATEGY: Using a Dictionary and a Glossary

Many textbooks include a glossary, that is, a list of important vocabulary and their meanings as they are used in the book. A dictionary and a glossary both give definitions of words; however, they are not exactly the same. A glossary usually has only definitions of technical words and concepts that the author thinks may be unknown to the students using the book. In addition, a glossary does not give all of the possible meanings of a word. It only gives the meaning(s) that are important in that textbook. Therefore, a glossary is very useful for technical words.

Although a glossary is usually easier to use than a dictionary (it has fewer words), it is not always possible to find all the words you need to look up. Many of the words that you do not know will not be technical words, and they will not be included in a glossary.

1. **Which of these words from Reading 1 would probably _not_ be included in the glossary for the textbook? Check (✓) them.**

   _____ 1. mental age

   _____ 2. standard

   _____ 3. standard deviation

   _____ 4. factors

   _____ 5. prestige

   _____ 6. nature/nurture issue

Many words have more than one meaning. Therefore, it is very important to choose the meaning that makes sense in context. (This is why bilingual dictionaries are not always helpful. There is often no way of knowing which of the translations is correct for a particular context.) However, dictionaries can give several clues to help you decide on the correct meaning.

These are

- the parts of speech
- the various definitions
- the sample sentences containing the word

First, find out the part of speech of the word you are looking for. It is not very helpful to look at the meanings of verbs if the word you need is used as a noun.

Next, read all of the definitions for the word with the part of speech you want and find one that makes sense in the context where you need it.

If you do not understand a definition, look at the sample sentence. Most dictionaries give a sample sentence for each meaning of a word. The sample sentence shows you how the word is actually used and can give you important clues about its meaning.

2. Which meaning is correct for these words from Reading 1? Look the words up in a dictionary. On the lines below, write the meanings in your own words.

1. abstract (paragraph 1) _____

2. standard (paragraph 6) _____

3. correlate (paragraph 11) _____

F. Building Your Vocabulary

Although it is possible to learn new words by studying a vocabulary list, it is not the only way, or even the most effective way of increasing your vocabulary. Another good way is by reading as much as you can. Studies show that most people have to see a word in eight to ten different places before they really learn it. Which of the new words in this reading are you likely to find only in texts about psychology or education? Which ones might you find in more general types of texts? Can you think of any words that you have learned from this book after seeing them over and over?

When you read a textbook, key words are often highlighted in some way. Look back at Reading 1. What are the key words? Write them in your notebook. Are there any other new words that you think will be helpful for Unit Task 1? Add them to the list in your notebook. Write the part of speech of the word. If you are not sure, look in a dictionary. Then, write a sentence for each new word. Do you think you can learn some of these key words if you continue to read and use them?

Look at the writing topics below. Choose at least one and write about it.

1. What qualities do you think are necessary for people to be happy and satisfied in their lives? Of these qualities, are there any that are more important than others? How does a person's intelligence relate to this?

2. Do you think that all children should be given an IQ test when they begin school? Explain the reasons for your opinion.

Step 3: Note Useful Information

When you are doing research on a topic, you may find texts which are useful as background information even if they are not directly related to your task.

Reread Unit Task 1. Is Reading 1 directly related to the task? Why or why not? If your answer is no, which ideas may be useful as background information? Go back to the text and highlight or underline them.

H. Making Connections

Look back at Reading 3 in Unit 3. What problems did Ritu's talent cause her family? Do you think that Ritu's special ice-skating ability and early development are related to her IQ? Why or why not?

READING 2: "GARDNER'S EIGHT INTELLIGENCES"

Step 1: Preview the Reading

1. **Reading 2 actually includes three different texts. What are they?**

2. **What is the homework for this class?**

3. **If you were a member of this class, what ideas do you think would be important for you to note in these texts? How are they different from the ideas that are important for Unit Task 1?**

4. **Look back at the list of questions you wrote in your notebook for Unit Task 1. Which questions do you think this article may answer? Put a check mark (✓) next to them.**

Step 2 : Read Closely

1. **Read the text. The first time you read, cover up the margin questions. Look for the answers to the questions you checked in your notebook. Write any answers that you find next to your questions.**

2. **Read the text again. Use the margin questions to help you.**

ASSIGNMENT:

Study the handouts on Gardner's eight intelligences and Carbo, Dunn and Dunn's learning styles. Be prepared to discuss the validity of both theories and how they relate to each other.

Do the global vs. analytical inventory. Do you think this is an accurate way to describe different ways of thinking?

READING 2A

1. How is this reading organized?

2. How does the format help you to understand the organization?

3. Can you get a general idea of the meaning of *sensations*?

4. What may help you to understand what type of thing a *maze* is?

GARDNER'S EIGHT INTELLIGENCES

Dr. Howard Gardner from Harvard University has identified the following intelligences:

1. **Linguistic Intelligence**
   People with this kind of intelligence understand and use language easily. They think logically and analytically. They enjoy reading and writing, memorizing information, talking and building their vocabularies (they are great spellers). They may also be excellent storytellers.

2. **Logical-Mathematical Intelligence**
   People with lots of logical intelligence are interested in patterns, categories and relationships. They are interested in arithmetic problems, strategy games, experiments and how things work. They often find unusual ways to solve problems, but they may not be able to explain how they did it.

3. **Bodily-Kinesthetic Intelligence**
   These people process knowledge through bodily sensations. They are often athletic; they may be dancers or good at crafts such as sewing or woodworking. They enjoy training their bodies to do their physical best. Having to sit for a long time is very uncomfortable for them.

4. **Visual-Spatial Intelligence**
   People with this type of intelligence think in images and pictures. They have a very good sense of direction and enjoy maps. They may be fascinated with mazes or jigsaw puzzles, or spend free time drawing, building things or daydreaming. People with strengths in this area have the most potential to be successful in new technological fields such as computers.

5. **Musical-Rhythmic Intelligence**
   Those with this kind of intelligence often sing or drum to themselves. They are usually quite aware of sounds that other people may miss. These people are often careful listeners.

6. Interpersonal Intelligence

People who have a lot of interpersonal intelligence are often leaders. They are good at communicating and seem to understand others' feelings and motives.

7. Intrapersonal Intelligence

These people may be shy. They understand themselves much better than others may understand them. They are highly motivated to be true to their goals and do not care very much about what other people think of them.

8. Naturalist Intelligence

People with a strong naturalist intelligence have an outstanding knowledge of things in the natural world, such as plants and animals. They also have the ability to see how things fit into different natural categories. They like to fish, garden, cook and carefully observe things.

READING 2B

5. Can you guess what *Drs.* means?

6. Is it difficult for visual learners to think logically, analytically, and sequentially?

LEARNING STYLES

1 Drs. Marie Carbo, Rita Dunn and Kenneth Dunn have described the following three styles of learning.
- auditory
- visual
- tactile-kinesthetic

2 **Auditory learners** are logical, analytical thinkers. They are comfortable with typical school tasks including analyzing sounds and numbers, following directions in order, and just "doing the right thing." They are usually successful in school. Much of what they learn is from listening to information that is presented to them in class.

3 **Visual Learners** learn best by seeing a visual representation of the material. They are global thinkers. They like to see "the big picture" rather than the details. They can learn to think logically, analytically and sequentially, but they must do this by working backwards from the whole to the parts.

4 **Tactile-kinesthetic learners** learn best when they can touch things or move while they are learning. Like visual learners, they are also global thinkers.

Educational Psychology 243
Dr. Edwin Moser

ARE YOU AN ANALYTICAL OR GLOBAL THINKER?

Read the list and decide what kind of thinker you are.

When it comes to...	Analytical thinkers usually prefer...	Global thinkers usually prefer...
1. Sound	silence for studying	some sound while studying
2. Light	bright light for reading/studying	very low light for reading/studying
3. Temperature	warmer temperatures, heavy clothes	cooler temperatures, lighter clothes
4. Furniture	studying at a desk or in a chair	studying on a bed or the floor
5. Time of day	learning in the morning; going to bed early	learning later in the day; staying up late
6. Mobility	sitting still for long periods of time	moving around all the time
7. Tasks	working on one job at a time until done	doing several jobs at the same time
8. Deciding	taking a long time to make decisions	being spontaneous about decisions; doing what seems "right"
9. Time	being on time	not worrying about being late
10. Perceiving	seeing things as they are at the moment; noticing details	seeing things as they might be; perceiving the whole; ignoring details
11. Planning	making lists for everything; planning far in advance	doing things when they feel like it; experimenting
12. Eating	eating breakfast and regular meals	skipping breakfast; snacking while learning
13. Remembering	remembering what has been spoken	remembering what has been experienced
14. Learning	working alone; being self-directed, independent	working in a group; discovering answers for themselves rather than being told the answers
15. Thinking	common test types (multiple-choice, true/false, essay)	opportunities to express themselves in other ways than writing

A. Checking Your Comprehension

Answer the questions about the readings. Write the answers in your notebook.

1. What is the difference between Reading 2A and 2B?

2. What is the relationship between Reading 2B and 2C?

3. Which combination of intelligence type and learning style type do people who are successful in school often have?

4. Will analytical or global thinkers probably adapt better to a traditional school environment? Which characteristics will help them the most?

B. Making Inferences

What inferences can you make about the reading? Answer the questions below.

1. What do you think is Gardner's opinion of IQ tests? Why?

2. Why do you think auditory learners do well in school?

3. Can people choose which kind of intelligence or which learning style they want to have?

4. Which intelligences do you think are necessary for each of these jobs? Complete the chart. An example has been done for you.

JOB	INTELLIGENCE TYPE(S)
1. bank teller	logical-mathematical intelligence
2. lawyer	
3. mechanic	
4. teacher	
5. doctor	
6. gardener	
7. architect	
8. ice skater	

C. Topics for Discussion

Discuss the following questions with your classmates.

1. How might knowing about Gardner's theory affect how a person feels about himself or herself?

2. Is it important for teachers to know about the theories of multiple intelligences and learning styles? Why or why not?

3. Do the quiz in Reading 2C. Which kind of thinker are you? Does this quiz seem accurate to you? Why or why not?

4. Do schools try to help visual and tactile-kinesthetic learners enough? Should they try to help them more? How?

D. Reading Strategies

READING STRATEGY:
More Practice Understanding Referring Words—*these/those*

In Unit 3 you learned about the referring words **this** and **that**. You learned that **this** and **that** can come before a noun or stand alone.

Gardner has a theory about intelligence. **This** theory says that...

The words **these** and **those** are used in the same way. Who does **these people** refer to in the lines below?

7. Intrapersonal Intelligence

These people may be shy. They understand themselves...

Look at two short texts below. Underline the referring words and phrases and write the words or ideas that they refer to. An example has been done for you. Hint: Do not forget the personal pronouns (*he, she, it, them, her, etc.*).

---

5. **Musical-Rhythmic Intelligence**
   people
   Those with this kind of intelligence often sing or drum to themselves.

   They are usually quite aware of sounds that other people may miss.

   These people are often careful listeners.

3 **Visual Learners** learn best by seeing a visual representation of the

   material. They are global thinkers. They like to see "the big picture"

   rather than the details. They can learn to think logically, analytically

   and sequentially, but they must do this by working backwards from

   the whole to the parts.

VOCABULARY STRATEGY: More Practice with Affixes

In previous units we learned that an affix can change the meaning or part of speech of a word. We also learned that a prefix (an affix at the beginning of a word) usually changes the meaning of the word, and a suffix (an affix at the end of a word) usually changes its part of speech.

What suffix must you add to change these nouns to adjectives? How does the spelling change?

music _____   space _____

person _____   logic _____

Reread the sections of Reading 2A on interpersonal intelligence and intrapersonal intelligence. Can you guess the meaning of the prefixes **inter-** and **intra-**?

Can you think of any other words with an affix (suffix or prefix) like the ones used above? Add them to the list below.

1. international   2. _____   3. _____   4. _____

Step 3: Note Useful Information

Readings 2A and 2B explain each type of intelligence and learning style. Summarize the most important features of each intelligence type and learning style by making a chart.

Intelligence type	Abilities	Activities they enjoy	Other information
1. linguistic	logical/analytical thinking	read, write	good storytellers
2.			
3.			
4.			
5.			
6.			
7.			
8.			

1. Fill in this chart with information on intelligence types from Reading 2A. An example has been done for you.

2. Make a similar chart about learning styles in your notebook. Compare your chart with your classmates'.

3. Does Reading 2C have information that will be helpful for Unit Task 1? If not, is it generally interesting? Why or why not?

F. Building Your Vocabulary

Use these steps to build your vocabulary with words from the reading.

1. Readings 2A and 2B are lists of different items. Which words in the lists are the most important to understand in order to do Unit Task 1? Add these words to the list in your notebook. Write a definition in your own words for each one. All of these words are the same part of speech. What is it?

2. Look back at the readings. Are there any other new words that you think will be helpful for Unit Task 1? Add them to the list. (Remember to add words that will be generally useful, too.) Write the part of speech for each word. If you are not sure, look in a dictionary. Then, write a sentence for each new word.

G. Writing Your Ideas

Look at the writing topics below. Choose at least one and write about it.

1. If you could choose to have any of the intelligences in the reading, which one would you choose? Why?

2. Choose a common type of work (for example, teacher, electrician, or secretary) and explain which type of intelligence would fit well with that job. Explain the reason for your answer.

3. Do you think it is possible for one person to have several intelligences? Why or why not? Explain.

4. Think about some people that you know well—your friends, your family. Which kinds of intelligences do they have? Give examples to support your opinions.

H. Making Connections

Compare Gardner's theory of intelligences from Reading 2 with the concept of IQ and IQ testing in Reading 1. What are the benefits and weaknesses of each approach to understanding intelligence?

Step 1: Preview the Reading

1. **This reading has three different styles of print. What is each style used for? How does the formatting help the reader understand the organization of the text?**

2. **Quickly read the introduction to find out what this reading is about. Can you restate it here in one sentence?**

   _____

3. **Look back at the list of questions you wrote in your notebook for Unit Task 1. Which questions do you think this article may answer? Put a check mark (✓) next to them.**

Step 2: Read Closely

1. **Read the text. The first time you read, cover up the margin questions. Look for the answers to the questions you checked in your notebook. Write any answers that you find next to your questions.**

2. **Read the text again. Use the margin questions to help you.**

READING 3

The
BRAIN
Gain

1   Some educators are challenging the traditional measures of intelligence such as IQ tests. One leader of this rebellion is Howard Gardner, Ph.D., a Harvard University psychologist who says that there are actually eight kinds of intelligence—linguistic, logical, musical, spatial, kinesthetic, intra-personal, interpersonal and naturalistic. He says that those who take advantage of their natural strengths can go far. Those who rely on their weaknesses probably won't have much success. Here Gardner gives the interviewer a few tips on using our inner genius.

2   _INT: Your theory says we're all just as smart as the brain surgeon that we met at a party. Can that possibly be true?_

    HG: Well, because he works with knives, I hope he has greater kinesthetic intelligence than you do. But the fact that a person has a high IQ

1. Who is asking the questions?

2. Who is answering them?

doesn't mean he's "smart." We need to ask, "smart in what?" You could be intelligent in school, in business or in the arts. Intelligence is really about using all of your abilities to do something well. What you are trying to do determines which intelligence is most important. For example, logical intelligence is highly valued in today's society, but naturalistic intelligence—the ability to read changes and indications in the environment—was the most important intelligence for thousands of years.

3   *INT: Doesn't IQ consider all those different abilities?*

HG: No. For instance, Ronald Reagan probably had 50 fewer IQ points than Jimmy Carter or Herbert Hoover, but he was a much more effective president than either. Why? Because he had greater linguistic and interpersonal intelligence. He could motivate people. A leader's success depends on his ability to tell inspiring stories and to make others believe them. I like to listen to Bill Clinton because he's a terrific storyteller.

4   *INT: So you're saying all of us are extremely brainy in some way?*

HG: Yes. All human beings are capable of high performance in something—if they use their strongest intelligences. Unfortunately, many people focus on their weaknesses.

For instance, the lawyer who writes excellent legal analyses may be terrible in court. He may see himself as a failure. The problem is that he is relying on his interpersonal intelligence which is probably only average. Meanwhile he is ignoring his high logical or even spatial intelligence. If he'd take advantage of his natural strengths, he'd succeed and be less frustrated.

5   *INT: What's the best way to find "hidden" intelligences?*

HG: Take a hard look at yourself and your history. Think of tasks that were easy and hard for you. Think about what they have in common. If you're doing extremely well in a particular facet of your career, look at it carefully. What skills do you use? Most important, listen to what others say about you. If someone says, "you draw well," or "you resolved that conflict easily," don't ignore it. Take it seriously. They're giving you the most reliable clues about your natural intelligences.   ■

3. Do you know the meaning of *inspiring?* Does it matter?

4. What part of speech is *brainy?* What does it probably mean?

5. In paragraph 5, what does the word *hard* probably mean in the first line of HG's response.

A. Checking Your Comprehension

Answer the questions about the readings on the lines below.

1. Define "intelligence" as Gardner uses it here. Explain it in your own words.

   _____

   _____

   _____

2. What three pieces of advice does Dr. Gardner give?

   _____

   _____

   _____

B. Making Inferences

What inferences can you make about the reading? Put a check mark (✓) next to all of the statements about the reading that are correct.

Dr. Gardner probably believes that...

_____ 1. each of us has only one of the eight intelligences.

_____ 2. some intelligences are more useful than others in today's society.

_____ 3. these intelligences are innate (inborn).

_____ 4. many people do not know which of these intelligences they have.

_____ 5. your IQ determines how successful you will be.

C. Topics for Discussion

Discuss the following questions with your classmates.

1. Do you believe Dr. Gardner's theory of multiple intelligences? Why or why not?

2. Can you think of any other intelligence types that you think Dr. Gardner should include in his list? What are they?

3. Are the "intelligences" that Dr. Gardner talks about here the same as a person's "skills" or "abilities"? Explain.

READING STRATEGY:
Understanding How Examples Support Important Ideas

A writer often uses examples to explain his or her ideas. The examples also often show which ideas the writer feels are the most important.

Look at the example given in this text:

…Intelligence is really about using all of your abilities to do something well. What you are trying to do determines which intelligence is most important. <u>For example, logical intelligence is highly valued in today's society, but naturalistic intelligence—the ability to read changes and indications in the environment—was the most important intelligence for thousands of years.</u>

What is this an example of?

    a. how we have to use all of our abilities to be successful in today's society

    b. how the intelligence that is most important is related to the type of society you live in

    c. how logical intelligence is related to naturalistic intelligence

---

Look at these examples from Reading 3 and explain what point about multiple intelligences they illustrate.

1. Ronald Reagan versus Jimmy Carter

    _____

    _____

    _____

2. Bill Clinton

    _____

    _____

    _____

3. a lawyer

    _____

    _____

    _____

Which section of Reading 3 will probably be most helpful in doing Unit Task 1? Why? Give your reason, then summarize this section in your own words in your notebook.

E. Building Your Vocabulary

When we learn new words, it is often useful to learn them in groups of words which have related meanings or relate to the same topic. This way, we will know several different ways to talk about a particular idea or topic. For example in this unit, many of the readings are about *intelligence*. Can you find some words which have meanings related to *intelligent* or *intelligence*? It doesn't matter if they are different parts of speech. It may also be helpful to include some words you already know, as long as they are related to the group of words.

1. **Here are a few examples of words with related meanings for one topic:**

   intelligent

   brainy

   smart

   Can you add any other words to this list?

2. **Do you think that knowing a group of words on this topic might be helpful for Unit Task 1? How? Can you think of any other categories of words in the readings in this unit which might be helpful for doing the Unit Task? Add these groups of words to your notebook. Write the part of speech of each word. If you are not sure, look in the dictionary. Then, write a sentence for each new word.**

F. Writing Your Ideas

Look at the writing topics below. Choose at least one and write about it.

1. Do you agree with Dr. Gardner that we are all "very brainy" in some way? Why or why not? Give examples to support your opinions.

2. Dr. Gardner says that Ronald Reagan was a more effective president than Jimmy Carter even though he had a lower IQ. Have you ever known anyone who was very intelligent but not very successful at his job? Explain.

3. What kinds of "intelligences" do you think will be useful in the future? Why? Explain.

Although this text also discusses Gardner's "intelligences," does it do this in the same way as Reading 2A? Is the list of the intelligences in this reading as detailed as the one in Reading 2A? Why or why not? Is this a weakness in the text or are the author's purposes different?

Unit Task 1:
Figuring Out Your Intelligence Type and Learning Style

Your first task in this unit is to decide what your own strengths and weaknesses are, especially in terms of Gardner's eight intelligences and the three different styles of learning as described in Readings 1–3.

In order to do this, you must do some introspection. That means you must look inside yourself and analyze your own thoughts, feelings, and abilities.

---

1. Complete the following steps to help you do Unit Task 1:

1. Make a list of five things that you think that you do well and enjoy doing. (Hint: Do not just think about things that you do in class. Consider all the activities that you do.)

_____

_____

_____

_____

_____

2. Make a list of five things that you feel are difficult for you or that you sometimes avoid doing.

_____

_____

_____

_____

_____

3. Ask several people who know you well what they think you do well. Write their answers below.

_____

_____

_____

_____

4. Put a check mark (✓) next to the items you listed in 1–3 that relate to some of Gardner's different intelligences.

5. Which two or three of Gardner's intelligences do you think you have more of?

_____

_____

_____

6. Which two or three intelligences do you think you have less of?

_____

_____

_____

7. Think of a time when you learned something very easily. What did you learn? How did you learn it? (Don't forget to include things you learned outside of class.)

_____

_____

_____

_____

8. Think of something that was very difficult for you to learn. What was it? How were you trying to learn it?

_____

_____

_____

_____

9. What do you think your learning style is?

_____

2. How do you think you can use this knowledge about your best learning styles? What could you do to develop your weaker intelligences? Share your ideas with your class.

PART B — UNIT TASK 2: EVALUATING YOUR SCHOOL EXPERIENCE

Identify the Information You Need

1. **Read the instructions for Unit Task 2 on page 198. Think about the information that you will need to do it. Write questions on the lines below that will help you to do Unit Task 2. You will need to get information about schools and about teachers.**

QUESTIONS ABOUT SCHOOLS

1. _____?

2. _____?

3. _____?

4. _____?

5. _____?

QUESTIONS ABOUT TEACHERS

6. _____?

7. _____?

8. _____?

9. _____?

10. _____?

2. **Compare your questions with your classmates' questions. Are there any questions that you want to add to your list? Copy your final list of questions into your notebook.**

3. **Now look ahead to Readings 4–6. Which of them might give you the answers to each question? Draw a chart like the one on page 70, exercise 3, into your notebook. Write the question numbers and the reading numbers on the lines.**

UNIT 4   *175*

Step 1: Preview the Reading

1. **Where does this text come from? Do you think it came from a book, magazine, Web site, or newspaper?**

2. **Who is the intended audience?**

3. **Read the first and last paragraphs. Then scan the subtitles. What do you think this reading will be about?**

4. **How is this text different from other texts that you have read on this topic? How does the intended audience affect the content and style of the article?**

5. **Look back at the list of questions you wrote in your notebook to do Unit Task 2. Which questions do you think this article may answer? Put a check mark (✓) next to them.**

Step 2: Read Closely

1. **Read the text. The first time you read, cover up the margin questions. Look for the answers to the questions you checked in your notebook. Write any answers that you find next to your questions.**

2. **Read the text again. Use the margin questions to help you.**

READING 4

1. How is the information in this paragraph different from information in Readings 2 and 3?

Finding the Smart
Part of Every Child

1 There's a quiet revolution taking place in classrooms all around the country. Its main idea? All children are smart, and the job of teachers and parents is to help children find the style of learning that uses their natural intelligence.

2 The teachers in these classrooms are putting the theory of multiple intelligences (MI) into practice. The MI theory was developed by Howard Gardner and his colleagues at Harvard University. The theory of Multiple Intelligences challenges traditional ideas about intelligence. It also questions the value of intelligence tests. MI researchers point out that traditional teaching and testing focus only on two of the seven[1] kinds of intelligence that people possess—language and logic skills. So children who don't learn in a

[1] In Gardner's first book he named only seven intelligence types. He more recently added the eighth.

2. What is the author's main point here?

3. How are paragraphs 5-11 organized?

style that depends on language and logic are called inadequate.

3 According to Thomas Armstrong, author of *Seven Kinds of Smart* (Plume), the children are fine but the teaching methods are inadequate. "In traditional education, we try to remake students to get them to learn in our way. In fact, we need to remake the way we teach so that it fits the students," he explains. "We need to recognize that different children learn in different ways and that all ways of learning are okay. Then we will really be in the business of education," he adds.

SMART WAYS CHILDREN LEARN

4 As the title of Armstrong's book suggests, there are seven styles of learning—seven distinct intelligences. Verbal abilities and logic skills, which are so important to the traditional teaching of reading, writing, and arithmetic, are just two of these intelligences. Armstrong calls these "word smart" and "logic smart." The five other intelligences, according to MI researchers, are equally important. When we ignore them we are asking children to work against their own intelligence rather than with it. So, the question for teachers and parents is this: How do we match children's learning styles to what is being taught? Let's look at the ways children learn and some ideas about how to direct them.

5 • **Word Smart.** Most teaching today is based on the expectation that children are word smart, meaning they learn by listening, reading, speaking, and writing. Parents of these children need only to encourage them to keep up with their assignments.

6 • **Logic Smart.** This way of learning, too, follows traditional teaching methods, using number facts and scientific principles, as well as observation and experimentation. Children who are logic smart respond well to questions starting with, "What if...." Parents might also suggest that these children draw diagrams and make other analytical aids for learning.

7 • **Picture Smart.** These children can understand much more when they visualize what they are learning, whether it is a math concept or a history lesson. Give your picture-smart child plenty of visual demonstrations, from simple homemade charts to museum visits, and ask her to draw as often as possible with her studies.

8 • **Music Smart.** You'll find that background music doesn't bother these chil-

Children who are *word smart* learn by listening, reading, speaking and writing.

The *self-smart* child learns his lessons by personalizing them.

4. What does the phrase *in fact* signal?

5. Explain what *people smart* means in your own words.

6. What is a *self-smart* child's special ability?

7. In paragraph 13, which children are being referred to?

dren. In fact, it helps them learn! Information presented rhythmically is very successful with music-smart children. Try clapping out anything that can be put to rhythm—multiplication tables, perhaps—and watch this child "get" it.

9 • **Body Smart.** The child who suddenly figures out today's lesson as he walks home from school probably has this kind of intelligence. He also needs plenty of hands-on opportunities for learning through performing in skits and other physical experiences. Be sure these children have breaks to stretch and move throughout the day to keep their learning focus sharp.

10 • **People Smart.** Group projects, which make children compare notes, discuss, and decide, are the best ways for people-smart children to learn. They are very sociable, and learning as part of a group is often the best way for them.

11 • **Self Smart.** Ask the self-smart child how a situation would feel to him and he'll understand the lesson immediately. This child is often accused of daydreaming when in fact, he is learning his lessons by personalizing them. What would it have been like to be a Civil War soldier or an explorer at the North Pole?

12 All children can use each of these learning styles but some are stronger than others. Students naturally use one or more of their stronger styles. Armstrong notes, too, that a learner's preferred style this year may change next year. "Two and three-year olds are body smart," he says as an example. "They learn by touching, feeling, and doing. As children grow and change, they develop other strengths."

13 Culture also influences which strengths are used. "Almost all cultures pass on knowledge musically from one generation to the next," Armstrong observes. In our culture, children learn their ABC's through song. As children get older, we use music less and less as a teaching tool. "That's sad for all children," says Armstrong, "but for some children, it becomes a real tragedy."

14 One last warning: Armstrong is concerned that MI could become another exercise in labeling. He claims that it would be a mistake to focus on one intelligence. "Calling a child an artistic learner or any of the other ones defeats the purpose of MI," he stresses. "Our goal is to expand, not limit, each learner's potential. Let children use their special gifts, but also encourage them to explore all of the intelligences. That's the road to discovery." □

A. Checking Your Comprehension

Answer the questions about the readings on the lines below.

1. Whose theory of intelligences is discussed in this reading?

   _____

2. Whose book is discussed in this reading?

   _____

3. Whose terminology (system of names) is used in this reading? Why?

   _____

4. What is the purpose of the footnote on page 176?

   _____

5. What advice does the author of Reading 4 give to parents?

   _____

B. Making Inferences

What inferences can you make about the reading? Answer the questions below.

1. Howard Gardner wrote a book on his theory called *Frames of Mind.* Why did the author of this text choose to focus on *Seven Kinds of Smart* by Thomas Armstrong instead of Gardner's book?

2. Does Armstrong think that children who are "body smart" should be encouraged to be more "music smart" or "self smart"?

3. Do you think that Armstrong believes that students should take a test that would measure how smart they are in each area? Why or why not?

C. Topics for Discussion

Discuss the following questions with your classmates.

1. Which of the readings, Reading 2 or Reading 4, explains multiple intelligences more clearly for you? Which one do you think is more related to Unit Task 2?

2 Which kinds of learning styles are emphasized in your English classroom? Can you think of any activities that would focus on some of the others?

READING STRATEGY: More Practice with Organization: Main Ideas

In Unit Three you learned that many readings have different levels of information—a main idea, important ideas, and supporting details. The main idea of a text is sometimes given in one statement. The main idea for Reading 4 is given in paragraph 1.

All children are smart, and the job of teachers and parents is to help children find the style of learning that uses their natural intelligence.

All of the information in the reading supports and/or explains this idea.

---

1. **Look back at Reading 4. Complete the organization chart by doing the steps below. An example has been done for you.**

   1. Write the main ideas on the lines.

   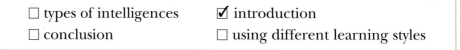

   | ☐ types of intelligences | ☑ introduction |
   | ☐ conclusion | ☐ using different learning styles |

   2. Write the most important idea of each paragraph in the boxes.

Introduction

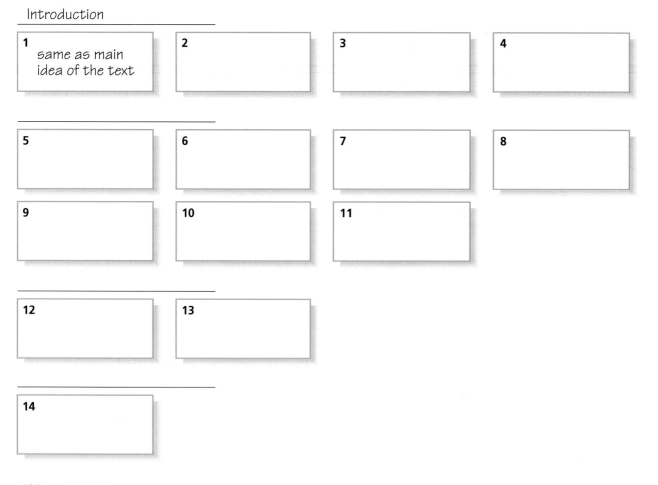

| 1 same as main idea of the text | 2 | 3 | 4 |

| 5 | 6 | 7 | 8 |

| 9 | 10 | 11 |

| 12 | 13 |

| 14 |

READING STRATEGY: More Practice with Referring Words

In previous units you learned that it is important to know what pronouns and other words refer to in a text. Look back at the Reading Strategy boxes on referring words on pages 66, 67, 107, and 165 to review this information.

2. **Complete the chart with the correct words. An example has been done for you.**

Referring word	Paragraph number	Refers to
1. it	2	theory of multiple intelligences
2. we	3	
3. these	4	
4. them	4	
5. this	4	
6. this	9	
7. that	14	

VOCABULARY STRATEGY:
More Practice with Suffixes— -(a)tion, -ize, -(ic)al

Look at these pairs of words. What does the suffix **-tion** or **-ation** do?

Good writers **organize** their ideas before they write. A clear **organization** helps readers to understand the writer's important ideas.

It is important to **connect** all the ideas in a text. This **connection** makes complicated ideas easier to understand.

All students are expected to **participate** in class discussions. You will receive a grade for your class **participation.**

Look at these pairs of words. What does the suffix **-ize** do?

I enjoy **social** occasions. I like to **socialize** with new people.

This factory is not very **modern.** They are going to **modernize** it next year.

Look at these pairs of words. What does the suffix **-al** or **-ical** do?

I am interested in Greek **culture.** I took a **cultural** tour last year.

We're studying **biology.** We're learning about **biological** warfare.

1. **Scan Reading 4. Find other words that end in *-tion* or *-ation* and write them in the chart. An example has been done for you.**

NOUN THAT ENDS IN *-(A)TION*	VERB ROOT
1. organization	organize
2.	
3.	
4.	
5.	
6.	

2. **Scan Reading 4. Find words that end in *-ize* and write them in the chart.**

VERBS THAT END IN *-IZE*	ADJECTIVE ROOT
1.	
2.	

3. **Scan Reading 4. Find other words that end in *-al* or *-ical* and write them in the chart.**

ADJECTIVES THAT END IN *-AL /-ICAL*	NOUN ROOT
1.	
2.	
3.	
4.	
5.	

Step 3: Note Useful Information

1. Some of the information in Reading 4 is not new. Which information is new? Much of this new information is about children. Will any of it be useful for Unit Task 2? How can you make it more useful?

2. Complete the chart with information from Readings 4 and 2. An example has been done for you.

Kind of smart from Reading 4	Intelligence type from Reading 2	Best ways to learn
1. word smart	linguistic intelligence	listening, speaking, reading, and writing
2.		
3.		
4.		
5.		
6.		
7.		

F. Building Your Vocabulary

Use these steps to build your vocabulary with words from the reading.

1. Gardner named his different intelligences in the following way:

   linguistic intelligence
   logical-mathematical intelligence
   bodily-kinesthetic intelligence
   visual-spatial intelligence

   musical-rhythmic intelligence
   interpersonal intelligence
   intrapersonal intelligence
   naturalist intelligence

   Compare these terms with the names Armstrong used. Which ones are more formal? Should you learn the formal or the informal names? What are benefits and drawbacks of each?

2. If you think it is important for you to know the formal names, you can still use the informal ones to help you understand what the others mean. In your notebook, write the informal name next to the formal one.

3. Look at Reading 4 again. Are there any other words that may help you with Unit Task 2? Add them to the list in your notebook. Remember to add words that will be generally useful, too. Write the part of speech for each word. If you are not sure, look in a dictionary. Then, write a sentence for each new word.

Look at the writing topics below. Choose at least one and write about it.

1. What kinds of activities did you enjoy doing in elementary school? Which ones did you not enjoy doing? Why?

2. Which kinds of "smart" does your culture encourage? Describe these and give some examples of how your culture teaches or encourages children to develop them.

H. Making Connections

The information given in Reading 4 is a little different from the information in Readings 2 and 3. Can you think of any possible reasons for these differences? Which text do you think is more accurate? How can you find out?

READING 5: "FACTORS THAT AFFECT STUDENT SUCCESS"

Step 1: Preview the Reading

1. Readings 5 and 6 are a continuation of Reading 1. Look back at the list of important vocabulary in Reading 1 on page 154. How many meanings do you remember? Scan Reading 1 for any special words that you cannot remember and reread those sections.

2. Now scan Reading 5 for the important words that were not explained in Reading 1. Circle the ones that you find.

3. Look back at the lesson overview and lesson objectives at the beginning of Reading 1. Underline the sections that apply to Reading 5.

4. Look at the title of Reading 5. Can you think of any factors that affect how well students learn?

5. Look back at the list of questions you wrote in your notebook for Unit Task 2. Which questions do you think this article may answer? Put a check mark (✓) next to them.

1. **Read the text. The first time you read, cover up the margin questions. Look for the answers to the questions you checked in your notebook. Write any answers that you find next to your questions.**

2. **Read the text again. Use the margin questions to help you.**

READING 5

1. Look at the format of this reading. How does it help you to understand the organization?

2. What is the purpose of the information between the dashes (——)?

3. What are the *reasons* that this sentence refers to?

4. What does the word *also* signal here?

FACTORS THAT AFFECT STUDENT SUCCESS

1   As was discussed earlier, IQ is a measurement of school performance, not a measure of intelligence. Now we will look at how different characteristics of schools can affect student success. We will begin with the basics of schooling, both the physical environment of the school and the school's educational philosophy.

PHYSICAL ENVIRONMENT

2   Most schools have many of the same characteristics—classrooms, hallways, a lunchroom, and a play yard—but they differ in other important ways. Some of these are classroom size, classroom arrangement, and number of children. Research has shown that overcrowded schools often have more problems with aggressive student behavior. Students fight with each other and sometimes even with their teachers. However, some schools find ways to manage overcrowding so that they have more cooperation and less aggression.

3   Research has also found that students in smaller schools have greater feelings of responsibility, competence, and challenge. In addition, children in smaller schools are more likely to be involved in extracurricular activities such as clubs and sports. For these reasons, smaller schools are often an aim of educational reform policies.

4   Class size is also important. Research has shown that classes with between twenty and forty students have about the same level of academic achievement. However, when the class is smaller than fifteen to twenty students there is an improvement in academic achievement. In the United States today the government is attempting to reduce class size from thirty-five to twenty-five students. According to the results found in research, this will probably not have any great effect on school performance.

EDUCATIONAL PHILOSOPHY
Traditional Classrooms

5   Educational philosophy also varies by school. The two most common philosophies are traditional classrooms and open classrooms. The traditional classrooms are far more common in the United States. In the traditional

classroom, the goal of schooling is to teach knowledge and standards of behavior that are valued by a culture. Children in these classrooms are mostly passive, not active. The teacher is an authority figure in the class. There is a standard set of expectations for children in each grade. In addition, children are compared to one another in order to be graded on their progress.

Open Classrooms

6   The goal of the open classroom approach is to create self-motivated learners. The goal of open classrooms is also to teach knowledge and standards of behavior that are valued by a culture. However, open classrooms also emphasize social and emotional development. In open classrooms, children are more active. Teachers are less authoritarian and often share the responsibility of decision making with the students. In this type of classroom, progress is made in a different way. Students are not compared to each other. Their present performance is compared to their earlier performance. The goal of the open classroom approach is to create self-directed learners who feel positive about themselves and others.

7   How do these two types of education compare? In general, it seems that open classrooms succeed in achieving their goals. Their students are more independent learners. Children in these classrooms also cooperate more effectively. There is no difference in self-esteem for students in open versus traditional classrooms. Also, on one of the most important measures, academic achievement, there is no advantage to an open versus traditional education. It is most likely that different people do well in different kinds of educational situations.

CLASSROOM ATMOSPHERE

5. What is the purpose of giving information about this study?

8   Are there other characteristics that make schools more or less effective for their students? Michael Rutter conducted a long term study in London on twelve secondary schools. These schools had low- and lower-middle-income students. The students took achievement tests when they started high school and again when they finished. In addition, Rutter looked at the characteristics of the schools. He found four factors that relate to effective schooling: student body composition, academic emphasis, classroom management, and discipline. In short, his results show that better organization, a clear focus on academic goals, and authoritative teachers all make for more effective education.

A. Checking Your Comprehension

1. Answer these questions about the reading.

1. What are the three major factors which affect a student's success in the classroom? Write them in your notebook.

2. What things are considered part of the physical environment at school?

   _____

3. What two main educational philosophies are discussed?

   _____

4. What four factors did Rutter find relate to effective schooling?

   _____

2. Compare open and traditional classrooms. Put a check mark (✓) in the correct column or columns. An example has been done for you.

	OPEN CLASSROOMS	TRADITIONAL CLASSROOMS
1. active students	✓	____
2. authoritarian teachers	____	____
3. children are compared with each other	____	____
4. more independent learners	____	____
5. each child's work is compared with his/her past work	____	____
6. effective learning environment	____	____
7. passive students	____	____
8. shared decision-making	____	____
9. students cooperate more effectively	____	____
10. knowledge and standards of behavior are taught	____	____

B. Making Inferences

What inferences can you make about the reading? Answer the questions below.

1. Is the writer probably more in favor of traditional or open classrooms? Why do you think so?

2. Which school is more likely to have an open classroom system—a large school or a small school?

3. Does the author value independent learning?

C. Topics for Discussion

Discuss the following questions with your classmates.

1. Which of the factors mentioned in the reading do you think is the most important for a school to be successful? Why?

2. Why do you think students at smaller schools are likely to be more involved in extracurricular activities?

3. Were any of the findings in Reading 5 new or unexpected for you ? Which? Why?

D. Reading Strategies

READING STRATEGY:
More Practice with Organization: Comparison/Contrast

You were introduced to comparison/contrast in Unit 1. This type of organization is used to show how two things are similar or different.

What is compared and contrasted in Reading 5 in paragraphs 2 and 3?

What is compared in paragraphs 5–7?

The information in comparison/contrast organization can be given in two different ways:

Organization 1

| Paragraph 1 | describes A |
| Paragraph 2 | describes B by comparing it to A |

Organization 2

Describes an aspect of A and describes the same aspect of B; describes another aspect of A and describes the same aspect of B; etc., point by point.

A	B
Aspect 1	Aspect 1
Aspect 2	Aspect 2
Aspect 3	Aspect 3

---

1. Answer these questions about Reading 5's organization.

1. Which type of organization is used in paragraphs 2 and 3?

   _____

2. Which type of organization is used in paragraphs 5 and 6?

   _____

3. Which type of organization is used in paragraph 7?

   _____

When a text compares two or more things, most of the important ideas will be given in those comparisons. Therefore, it is important to recognize the language of comparison. Look at some of the different kinds of expressions we can use.

For example:

Research has shown that overcrowded schools often have **more problems** with aggressive student behavior.

...children in **smaller schools** are **more likely** to be involved in extracurricular activities...

Teachers are **less authoritarian...**

However, there are many other ways of expressing comparisons. Some of these show similarity.

For example:

There is **no difference in** self-esteem for students in open versus traditional education.

The phrase **no difference in** is also used to compare the two types of education.

Sometimes the comparison involves more than one sentence.

...progress is made in a **different way.** Students are not compared to each other. Their present performance is compared to their earlier performance.

2. **Look back at Reading 5 and underline the other words and phrases that are used to compare open and traditional classrooms. Then, write them into the chart below. Check (✓) if they show a difference or a similarity. An example has been done for you.**

WORD/PHRASE	DIFFERENCE	SIMILARITY
no difference in		✓

3. **Which of the words and phrases you found above introduce important ideas?**

VOCABULARY STRATEGY: Understanding Complex Noun Phrases

A noun phrase is a noun and all of the words that describe it. The noun phrase in the following sentence is underlined.

<u>The player who was injured</u> left the game.

There is another way to say the same thing, however:

The injured player left the game.

In this case the noun phrase consists of three words—**the injured player.**

Academic and technical texts often use the second type of structure. This is one of the features that can make these kinds of texts more difficult to read. Therefore it is very important to learn to understand this structure.

Nouns in academic and technical texts also often have more than one word which describes them. Look at this example:

educational reform policies

Policies is the main noun. However, **educational reform** is another noun phrase which describes **policies. Reform** is the noun and **educational** is the adjective.

In other words, **educational** tells you which kind of **reform**, and **educational reform** tells you which kind of **policies**.

Here is another noun phrase from Reading 5:

Noun Phrase	Meaning
self-motivated learners	learners who are self-motivated (independent)

1. **What are the meanings of the noun phrases below? An example has been done for you.**

NOUN PHRASE	MEANING
1. student body composition	the types of students who are in the school
2. aggressive student behavior	
3. classroom size	
4. self-directed learners	

2. **Look back at Readings 1 and 5. Can you find any other examples of complex noun phrases? Write them on the lines below.**

_____

_____

_____

Step 3: Note Useful Information

Often the formatting of a text can help guide you to important information. Look at the subtitles of Reading 5. How will they help you find useful information for Unit Task 2?

E. Building Your Vocabulary

Do Exercise 1 or 2, or a combination of the two.

1. What are the two most important concepts in Reading 5? Write them in your notebook and write an explanation in your own words. Are there any other new words that you think will be helpful for Unit Task 2? Add them to the list in your notebook. Write the part of speech of the word. If you are not sure, look in a dictionary. Then, write a sentence for each new word.

2. If you are a visual learner, you might want to try to draw pictures which illustrate some of the different ideas in the text. For example, you might draw pictures like this to illustrate these words:

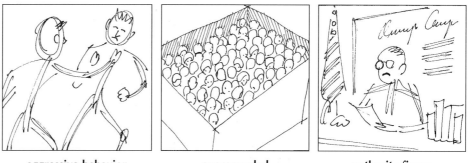

aggressive behavior   overcrowded   authority figure

Look back at the reading. Which words are important? Draw pictures for each one that you can. Do not forget to write the part of speech and a sentence for each one.

F. Writing Your Ideas

Look at the writing topics below. Choose at least one and write about it.

1. Do you have more experience with traditional or open classrooms? Which one do you prefer? If you have only experienced one, do you think you would like the other? Why or why not?

2. In what ways do you think schools in your country or community could be improved? Explain. Give reasons for your ideas.

G. Making Connections

How does Reading 5 relate to Reading 1? Do they support or contradict each other? Explain.

Step 1: Preview the Reading

1. Scan Reading 6 for more important words that were not in Reading 1 or 5. Circle the ones that you find.

2. Look back at the lesson overview and lesson objectives that were given in Reading 1. Double underline the parts of the overview and objectives that apply to Reading 6.

3. Look back at the list of questions you wrote in your notebook for Unit Task 2. Which questions do you think this article may answer? Put a check mark (✓) next to them.

Step 2: Read Closely

1. Read the text. The first time you read, cover up the margin questions. Look for the answers to the questions you checked in your notebook. Write any answers that you find next to your questions.

2. Read the text again. Use the margin questions to help you.

READING 6

MORE FACTORS IN STUDENT SUCCESS
TEACHER EXPECTATIONS

1. What is the main idea of paragraph 1?

1 In addition to the school atmosphere, the teacher greatly influences the child's learning experience. In fact, once they reach school age, children spend almost as much time with their teachers as they do with their parents. Teachers quickly form opinions of each student's future abilities and these expectations often affect the children's progress.

2. What is the main idea of paragraphs 2–4?

2 In a controversial study, researchers gave students in one school an IQ test. Then, they told teachers that the test showed that five children would "bloom" academically in the coming year. This was not actually true, however. The researchers had chosen the five children at random. At the end of the year, they gave the children another IQ test. In this test, the five children who had been called "bloomers" showed significant gains in IQ (15 points) and reading ability. In other words, children who were *expected* to do well did better than other students with the same ability.

3 How do teachers communicate their expectations to students? The method is shown in very small ways that teachers may not even notice. Think about what a teacher does when a "good" student gives a wrong answer. The teacher will often repeat the question using different words. This gives the student another opportunity to get the right answer. Then, the student receives praise for giving the correct answer. In this way, the teacher shows the student that he can overcome failure by trying harder.

3. Why does the author give these examples? What idea do they help to explain?

4 However, the same teacher may react differently when a "poor" student gives a wrong answer. Very often, this student is not given the opportunity to give the right answer. He is simply told, "No, that's wrong, does anyone else know the answer?" In this way, the teacher suggests to the student that his failure is because of a lack of ability. This second example can lead to a feeling of learned helplessness on the part of the student.

LEARNED HELPLESSNESS VS. MASTERY ORIENTATION

4. What words and phrases are used to compare these two ideas?

5 Learned helplessness and its opposite, mastery orientation, refer to the way children think about their own success and failure. In **learned helplessness,** a student who fails at a task believes that her failure is because of a lack of ability. The child who has a **mastery orientation** more often believes that when she succeeds it is because she has ability and when she fails it was because she didn't try hard enough.

6 The difference is in how the child will respond to failure. In the case of learned helplessness, the child thinks that he failed because he lacks ability; therefore there is no reason to try harder. In a sense, if the student has a feeling of learned helplessness, failure at a certain task means defeat. In a child with mastery orientation, a failure is often explained as a lack of effort rather than a lack of ability. In this case, the child feels that he has the ability, and he thinks that if he tries harder, he will succeed.

5. What is the purpose of paragraphs 7–8?

7 In a famous study, Carol Dweck and her colleagues researched learned helplessness and sex differences in the classroom. These researchers found that teachers treat boys' and girls' failures differently. In part, this is probably because teachers view boys' and girls' behavior differently. In general, teachers criticize boys more for bad behavior in class and effort-type failures, such as sloppy work, or lateness.

8 Girls are generally seen as better behaved. Therefore, girls are more often criticized for ability-related failures, such as wrong answers. Girls who have this experience may then begin to feel like they do not have the ability to do well. Boys, on the other hand, are criticized for a lack of effort, and then praised for getting the right answer. This leads boys to believe that they have the ability to succeed if they only work harder. This pattern in sex differences in learned helplessness and teacher expectations has been studied more completely, and it may turn out to be especially important in how girls respond to math classes in high school, which are culturally considered to be a subject in which boys do better.

9 Learned helplessness does not only affect girls, because the teacher behaviors that lead to a sense of learned helplessness have to do with what teachers expect from their students. This may help explain the results of the academic "bloomers" study described earlier. When teachers have high expectations of a student, they may unknowingly assist in that student's

progress, while similarly hindering the progress of a low-expectancy student. Thus, it becomes important to know how teachers form expectations of their students.

10 Different children in the same classroom receive very different educations. In general, teachers in America expect lower-income children to do more poorly than higher-income students and cultural minority[4] children to do worse than other children. Research has shown that teachers of low-income children make three times as many negative comments to their students as teachers of middle-income students. Even before teachers have academic information about students, they might place children in "ability" groups based on their neatness, clothing quality, and use of standard English. All of these factors play a role in the academic performance of children in school, and they may be very important for understanding how different children even in the same classroom receive very different educations.

FAMILY AND SOCIAL FACTORS

6. How many factors are listed here?

11 In addition to the importance of teacher expectations, parents also affect how a child does in school. Parental education, belief in the importance of schooling, and involvement in the child's education all have effects on the child's academic performance. Research has shown that although schooling is valued just as highly in lower- and middle-income homes, in lower-income homes the expectations of academic success may be lower.

12 Another factor that can affect children in different ways is how educational materials relate to a child's personal experience. In the United States, textbooks and what schools choose as "culturally relevant" are generally centered around the lives and experiences of middle-income non-minority students. These experiences may not be as relevant to the lives of many minority students. Research has shown that minority students who do more poorly in reading and writing than their classmates often do not show the same achievement gap in mathematics.

Research has shown that minority students who do more poorly in reading and writing than their classmates often do not show the same achievement gap in mathematics.

[4] A small group in a community or a country that differs from the larger part of the population in race, religion, culture, language, etc.

A. Checking Your Comprehension

Answer the questions about the reading on the lines below.

1. How do teacher expectations affect a student's success?

   _____

2. Which groups do teachers often believe are more able to succeed than others?

   _____

3. Which groups do teachers often consider less able to succeed than others?

   _____

4. Explain the concept of "learned helplessness" in your own words.

   _____

5. Explain the concept of "mastery orientation" in your own words.

   _____

6. How are girls and boys treated differently in the classroom?

   _____

7. What family factors may affect a student's success?

   _____

B. Making Inferences

What inferences can you make about the reading? Answer the questions below.

1. What are teachers' expectations of boys' behavior in the classroom?

2. What are teachers' expectations of girls' behavior in the classroom?

3. What are society's expectations of girls' ability in mathematics?

4. Why does the author think cultural minority students often have lower scores than other students in reading but not in mathematics?

C. Topics for Discussion

Discuss the following questions with your classmates.

1. If something is "controversial" it is likely to cause people to disagree. Why do you think the study discussed in paragraph 2 was controversial?

2. Do the examples of how teachers react to "good" and "bad" students seem correct in your experience? Can you think of any reason(s) why teachers might react this way?

3. Do you believe that teachers can affect how students feel about their ability to learn? Why or why not? How important is the teacher in a child's learning experience?

D. Reading Strategies

READING STRATEGY:
More about Referring Words: Sexism and Pronouns

As you have probably already learned, English has different pronouns for females *(she, her)* and for males *(he, him)*. However, there is no neutral pronoun which can be used to describe an unknown person (who may be male or female) when making a general statement. Traditionally, the pronouns *he* and *him* have been used when no particular person is being referred to. Some people are not happy with this system. They feel that females are not included when we use just the male pronouns. Therefore, some writers use other ways of referring to an unknown person. One way is to include both males and females by writing *he or she,* or *him/her.* Other writers choose to use only the female forms *she* and *her* all the time or to alternate the male and female pronouns each time. Another way is to avoid using any singular pronoun completely by using a plural form (for example, *they*) or by using a noun phrase instead of a pronoun (for example, *this child*).

Look at the following paragraphs from Readings 4 and 6 in this unit. Which pronoun(s) did the author use in each case?

1. Reading 6, Paragraph 1, referring to *children*   _____

2. Reading 6, Paragraph 4, referring to a *student*   _____

3. Reading 6, Paragraph 5, referring to a *student*   _____

4. Reading 6, Paragraph 9, referring to a *teachers*   _____

5. Reading 4, Paragraph 7, referring to a *picture-smart child*   _____

6. Reading 4, Paragraph 8, referring to a *music-smart child*   _____

7. Reading 4, Paragraph 9, referring to a *body-smart child*   _____

8. Reading 4, Paragraph 11, referring to a *self-smart child*   _____

What is the effect of using pronouns in each of these ways? What is your opinion of each one?

VOCABULARY STRATEGY: Using a Vocabulary Decision Tree

By now you have learned many different ways of dealing with unknown vocabulary. One possible way of putting them in a logical order is to use a vocabulary decision tree like the one below.

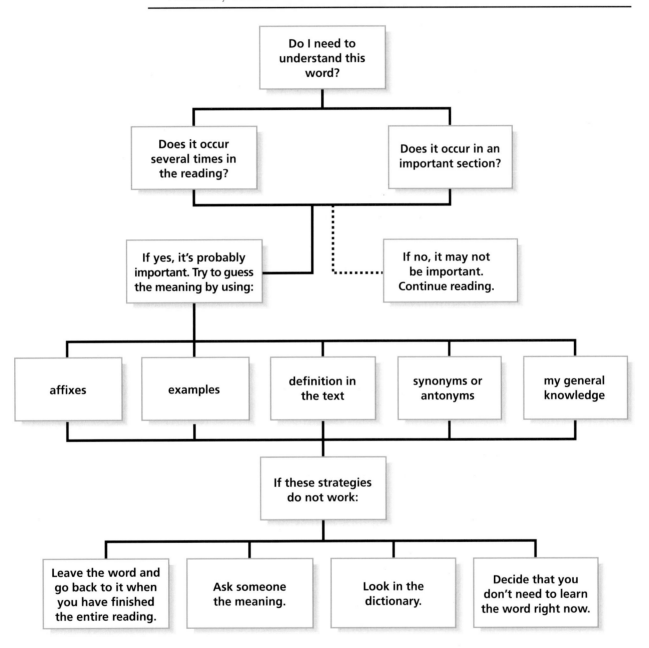

Find five words in Readings 1–6 that you still do not understand. Use the decision tree to decide how to deal with them. Explain your decisions to a partner. Does your partner agree with you?

Look back at the reading and make a list in your notebook of the factors that affect a student's success in school. Which ones can you connect to your own school experience? How did they occur in your life? Put a check mark (✓) next to the ones that you think had the most effect on you.

F. Building Your Vocabulary

Use these steps to build your vocabulary with words from the reading.

1. What two words or expressions are the most important for Unit Task 2 in this reading? Write them in your notebook.

2. Are there any other new words that you think will be helpful for Unit Task 2? Add them to the list in your notebook. Remember to add words that will be generally useful, too. Write the part of speech of the word. If you are not sure, look in a dictionary. Then, write a sentence for each new word.

G. Writing Your Ideas

Look at the writing topics below. Choose at least one and write about it.

1. Have you ever felt that a teacher had especially high or low expectations of you? How did it make you feel? Did it affect how much you were able to learn?

2. How should a teacher deal with a student who is having a hard time in his or her class? What suggestions do you have?

3. Have you ever taken a class in which you did very well? Have you ever taken one that was very difficult for you? Think about the ways that the teachers treated you. How were they the same? How were they different?

UNIT TASK 2:
Evaluating Your School Experience

For this task, you will evaluate your elementary school experience (grades 1–6), using the information in Readings 4–6. If you cannot remember enough about your elementary school or would rather not write about your own experience you can:

• write about your high school experience
• write about the school experience of someone that you know
• write about schools in your country in general

Although you will do the final activity individually, it may be helpful to work in groups in order to share experiences and ideas.

You may do this task as a written or oral report.

Complete the following steps to help you do Unit Task 2:

1. Think about the physical characteristics of your elementary school (e.g. Were the classes large or small? Were the classrooms light or dark? etc.). Make a list of anything that you can remember. Share your list with other members of your group.

   a. _____

   b. _____

   c. _____

   d. _____

   Look at your list and check (✓) any of the characteristics that are mentioned in the readings.

2a. Think about your elementary school experience. When did you do the best or learn the most? Write anything that you can remember about the teacher(s) who seemed the most effective. How did they treat you? How did they treat the other students in the class?

   _____

   _____

   _____

   _____

   _____

2b. Is there any information in the readings that might help you to understand why the teacher(s) treated you this way?

   _____

   _____

   _____

   _____

3a. When did you do poorly or learn the least? Write anything that you can remember about the teacher(s) who seemed the least effective. How did they treat you? How did they treat the other students in the class?

   _____

   _____

   _____

   _____

   _____

3b. Is there any information in the readings that might help you to understand why the teacher(s) treated you this way?

_____

_____

_____

_____

_____

4. Are there any other factors mentioned in the readings that you feel relate to your elementary school experience?

_____

_____

_____

_____

_____

5. How has your elementary school experience affected your attitudes toward learning?

_____

_____

_____

_____

_____

6. Finally, prepare your written or oral report for your class.

PART C   EXPANSION ACTIVITIES

Applying Your Knowledge

1. Interview a teacher from an elementary school. Find out about the school's educational philosophy.

2. Observe several elementary school classes. Do the teachers treat the students in the ways mentioned in the readings?

The Electronic Link

Do an Internet search. Use the words *education, learning,* and *school systems.*

What sites did you find? Compare your answers with those of your classmates.

Now choose one Web site and fill in the information below.

Name of site: _____

URL (Web address): _____

What state or country is this site from? _____

What did you learn about education and learning by looking at this site?

_____

_____

Is there any information on this site that you agree with? Disagree with?

_____

_____

For More Information

National Association of University Women
1001 E Street NW
Washington DC 20003
http://www.libertynet.org/nauw/index.html

National Education Association
1201 16th Street NW
Washington DC 20036
http://www.nea.org

📖 **See the Additional Readings for this unit on pages 214–217.**

Essay Questions

Choose one of the topics below and write an essay about it.

1. Some people are critical of Howard Gardner's work because they say that some of his "intelligences" are physical abilities rather than true intelligence. How do you feel? Should the definition of intelligence be limited to thinking ability?

2. How important is it that students learn information that is relevant to their culture or their socio-economic group? Do you believe that this is an important factor in learning? Why or why not?

Evaluating Your Progress

Think about the skills and strategies that you used in this unit. Check (✓) the correct boxes.

	NEVER	SOMETIMES	OFTEN	ALWAYS
1. I was able to use the elements of a textbook to preview and read more efficiently.	☐	☐	☐	☐
2. When I previewed, I thought about where a reading came from and what I knew about the topic.	☐	☐	☐	☐
3. I was able to figure out the important ideas in a reading.	☐	☐	☐	☐
4. I was able to recognize the type(s) of organization used in a reading.	☐	☐	☐	☐
5. I was able to understand why the writer used particular examples.	☐	☐	☐	☐
6. I looked up words in the dictionary only when absolutely necessary.	☐	☐	☐	☐
7. When I looked up a word in the dictionary, I was able to choose the correct meaning.	☐	☐	☐	☐
8. As I read, I was careful to notice referring words and think about what they referred to.	☐	☐	☐	☐
9. I was able to use affixes to help me guess the meanings of new words.	☐	☐	☐	☐
10. I thought about parts of speech when I was trying to figure out the meaning of unknown words.	☐	☐	☐	☐

Setting Your Reading Goals

1. Choose three items from the list on page 202 that you would like to improve. Write them below.

   Goal #1 _____

   Goal #2 _____

   Goal #3 _____

2. Look back at your reading goals from Unit 3 on page 149. Are you moving toward these goals? Which ones still need more work?

1. AN ENGAGEMENT ANNOUNCEMENT

Rebecca Winslow Sawyer to wed Robert Graham Crowley

Mrs. Charlotte Winslow Sawyer of Grosse Point, Michigan announces the engagement of her daughter, Rebecca, to Mr. Robert Graham Crowley of Hillsboro, Illinois. Ms. Sawyer is also the daughter of the late Reginald Sawyer, founder and former CEO of Sawyer Communications. She is a recent graduate of Harvard University's MBA program and currently works in the head office of Sawyer Communications. Mr. Robert Crowley is the son of Henry and Violet Crowley of Hillsboro, Illinois. Mr. Crowley is also employed at Sawyer Communications. An April wedding is planned.

2. A JOB OFFER

BAY AREA SYMPHONY ORCHESTRA
SAN FRANCISCO, CALIFORNIA

Thomas Yamaguchi: MUSIC DIRECTOR   Sarah Lindstrom: ASSISTANT CONDUCTOR

May 27, 1998

Dear Lydia,

I have heard a rumor that you plan to retire from touring. It seems hard to believe considering how successful you have been; however, if it is true, it comes as great news to us at the Bay Area Symphony. As you know, Rudolph Percochek, has decided to retire so we will be looking for a world-class musician to take the first violinist position. If you do decide to retire from touring, and would consider taking a symphony position, I would like to invite you to come and play with us for a week in the fall. That would help you and us to see if such an alliance would be to our mutual benefit.

Please let me know what you think.

Sincerely,

Tom

3. YOUR MONEY

MAKING A WILL COULD CHANGE THE LIVES OF YOUR LOVED ONES

A will is an all-important document — and yet too few people, especially women, have one. "I don't have anything to leave; I'll do it when I've got some time; my husband has a will," are the excuses that are often heard.

I can't emphasize enough the importance of having a will. Dying without a will is selfish. It leaves your family with a financial mess to clear up, and even worse, it could leave your children under the care of someone you do not approve of.

Having a will lets you decide on the distribution of your earthly goods — like who gets your car, your favorite ring and your not-so-favorite bracelet.

If you die without a will, that is, intestate, your goods will be distributed according to the law. In general this means the goods are shared between the surviving spouse and children, and if there aren't any, they go back one generation to the parents.

You don't have to be rich to have a will — if you have items you'd like to leave to certain people then you should write a will. You may be surprised, when adding up your balance sheet, at exactly how much you have to give away.

To my mind, by far the most important reason to have a will is to ensure the well-being of your minor children. This is particularly important in cases where you are the only surviving parent, because if you die intestate, the court will decide where your children should go.

By nominating a legal guardian, you determine who will take over your legal parental power and look after the financial interests of your children until they reach majority. If you wish, you can divide these two duties. That is, you can give one person custody of the children and another the guardianship. The person with custody takes care of the children on a day to day basis. The person with guardianship is in charge of finances.

A married woman should have her own will. Some years ago, joint wills were popular among married couples, but these can cause practical difficulties when winding up the estate of the spouse who dies second.

A married couple should know the contents of each other's will, and be aware of the financial implications.

Next week we'll look at the practical considerations of writing a will: who to go to for advice, the minimum legal requirements, the executor's fee and tips on what should and should not go into your last testament.

By Amy Peters

1. SHORTCUTS

FUN FINDING FLAWS IN FILMS

Some people go to the movies to be entertained. Bill Givens goes to the movies to find mistakes. Givens is the author of *Roman Soldiers Don't Wear Watches: 333 Film Flubs—Memorable Movie Mistakes* (Citadel Press, 1996), which points out various mistakes that include lapses of logic, shots of the crew, odd noises and problems in chronological sequences. (The title is taken from one of the more well-known movie blunders: in some historical films that used extras by the hundreds in battle scenes, a few can be seen with their wristwatches still on.)

Some of the goofs may even make you rent the films to see the mistakes yourself. What is the point of all this? Movie-makers and movie stars are human too—what a comforting thought.

A sampling of some of the better flubs:

- In *Forrest Gump* (1994), "Robin Wright shows Tom Hanks a clipping in a scrapbook, which says 'USA Today, 1978.' USA Today began publication in 1982."

- "In *Spartacus* (1960) You can see more than one soldier charging up a hill wearing tennis shoes."

- "When one of the hit men in the crazy comedy *A Weekend at Bernie's* (1989) was knocked out and dragged into a closet, he conveniently lifted his feet so the closet door could shut."

- "Michael Douglas starred with Danny DeVito in *War of the Roses* (1989). As they look at papers on a desk, Douglas looks up and says, 'No, no, DeVito!' "

- "John Wayne was a busy man being both star and director of *The Alamo* (1960). Maybe that is why he didn't notice that mobile trailers appear in the background of several battle scenes... or that we can see a stuntman fall and land on a mattress?"

- A reporter thrusts a tape recorder in Harrison Ford's face as he leaves the courthouse in *Presumed Innocent* (1990). "You can see that there's no cassette in it; the recorder is empty."

By Jeannine Stein. Copyright, 1997, *Los Angeles Times*.

2. KING KONG IS STILL THE MASTER OF THE AMERICAN PSYCHE

It's the classic story of beauty and the beast, of attraction and repulsion between babe and brute.

He's big, hairy and uncouth, a grunting galoot who refuses to keep his paws off women. It seems we can't let go of him either.

King Kong, the master of the jungle and one of the granddaddies of movie monsters, has reached retirement age, turning 65 this month, yet his grip on our psyche and our pocketbook has rarely been stronger.

Disney is planning a year-end release for its big-budget homage to *Mighty Joe Young*, Kong's poorer cousin.

Music stores are stocked with a reissue of the original 1933 *King Kong* soundtrack. Legions of fans are charting expeditions to Monroeville, Pa., June 19 through 21 for a celebration of Kong, his creators and his movies. And Universal Studios continues to wrestle with its on-again-off-again Kong remake, which executives hoped would stomp into theaters this year.

Why the enduring interest in the big ape? Academics cite the "myth of the sentient monkey," the belief in a feeling, humanlike gorilla, but the rest of us can peel it down to something more basic: sex.

King Kong is the classic story of beauty and the beast, of attraction and repulsion between babe and brute, of colossal male strength neutralized by the power of feminine love.

Kong's death scene atop the Empire State Building, where he gazes at his beloved blond goddess before falling to the street, is American folklore.

Today, Kong's roar echoes through blockbusters such as *Jurassic Park* and *The Lost World*. While not the first giant creature to fill the big screen, he is the most influential.

The special effects that brought him to life were the marvel of their day — painstaking, stop-motion photography in which small models were filmed on miniature sets. And even now, advertisers use him to sell everything from insurance to plane tickets to newspapers.

Kong has survived a fight to the death with Godzilla, an awful 1976 Dino DeLaurentiis remake (starring an unknown Jessica Lange) and a cartoon series that portrayed him as an overgrown house pet battling social injustice along with prehistoric dinosaurs.

Film historians say *King Kong* is a prism through which we sense wild fantasies and dark nightmares, an American classic that resonates across time and generations.

"The closing line of that movie has always enraged me, 'It was beauty killed the beast,'" said Alison Scott, head of the pop-culture library at Bowling Green State University in Ohio. "I always want to scream, 'It was greed!'"

Scott says *King Kong* may be among the first cinematic depictions of man's inhumanity to nature: Modern man travels to an unspoiled land, abducts a wild animal and introduces it to the civilized world. When mayhem ensues, the creature gets the blame and the punishment — death.

Some see Kong as a metaphor for the Depression, an enormous, unstoppable monster wrecking the center of capitalist America, New York. (As the film opens, Fay Wray's Ann Darrow is about to faint from hunger as she filches an apple from a cart.) Others say Kong is a symbol of the adolescent male — tormented by sexual desires, cursed by an outsized awkwardness and plagued by unsightly, sprouting hair.

Despite his ferocity, not to mention a yen for munching on villagers, Kong emerges as a sympathetic victim, half of an archetypal romance between mismatched lovers.

"It's an essential American movie, and it speaks to American culture in all kinds of ways," said Jack Nachbar, co-editor of the Journal of Popular Film and Television. "There's elements of the sexual, of limits of power, of the primitive versus the technically complex... It's entered the American — or maybe the world — realm of references."

The producers promised Fay Wray that her co-star would be "the tallest, darkest leading man in Hollywood." They didn't mention he was an ape.

Two and a half years in the making, *King Kong* opened in New York on March 2, 1933, playing 10 times a day at the Roxy and Radio City Music Hall and setting world records for attendance. The film grossed $89,931 in four days, a fortune in an era when tickets cost about 15 cents.

The plot was simple: An adventurous movie producer travels to a mysterious island to film the elusive native deity known as Kong. His leading lady, beautiful Ann Darrow, is kidnapped by the natives and offered as a sacrifice to the ape, who falls in love with her.

Sailors rescue Darrow and capture Kong, spiriting him to New York. There, Kong bursts from his chains and rampages through the city, snatching Darrow and climbing the Empire State Building. Navy planes blast away at the ape, who carefully places Darrow on a ledge before falling to his death.

"Fay Wray says Kong is the ultimate outsider, that he's misunderstood, and everyone can associate with that," said Boyd Campbell, a Mississippi movie writer and *King Kong* authority. "I think she's probably right. Visually he's big and impressive, but he's also very human."

Kong himself was not one ape but six — all 18-inch models, covered in rabbit fur. His roar came from recording lions and tigers, mixing their growls, then slowing the tape and playing it backwards.

Originally titled "The Beast" and then "The Eighth Wonder," the movie cost $672,000, more than three times the average price of a 1933 picture. Producer-directors Merian Cooper and Ernest Schoedsack saved money by borrowing used sets. The swamp, waterfalls, and cliffs of Skull Island came from *The Most Dangerous Game*, while the native village belonged to *Bird of Paradise*.

The film has its peculiarities. Olympic champion Jim Thorpe appears as one of the native dancers; he was moonlighting as a movie extra to earn a few bucks. And Kong grows six feet during his trip from jungle to city.

By the time he reached New York, Kong stood 24 feet. Promotional posters claimed Kong was more than twice as tall — at that height Wray would have disappeared into his paw — but he was nonetheless huge and disturbing.

So disturbing that censors cut five scenes from the film's 1933 rerelease, including one of Kong stripping Wray, tickling her and then smelling his fingers. Another showed the ape crushing a villager as if the man were a cigarette. Particularly upsetting was the scene in which Kong, searching for his lost love, plucks the wrong woman from her apartment, realizes his mistake, and casually drops her to the street.

Most of the excised segments were restored in 1971. One remains a lost, holy grail of Kongophiles: a sequence in which sailors on Skull Island are devoured by giant spiders, a scene so grisly that it made many patrons at a 1933 preview walk out. "It stopped the picture cold, so the next day back at the studio, I took it out myself," director Cooper said in later interviews.

He and his partner Schoedsack cast themselves as two of the fighter pilots, reasoning that since they put Kong on top of the Empire State Building, they should be the ones to take him down. By the time Kong hits the pavement, there isn't a dry eye in the house, so thoroughly empathetic a character has he become.

The new *Mighty Joe Young* is the most ambitious film Disney has ever made, say studio executives. The smaller, gentler ape makes his encore this fall, 49 years after his debut.

Universal Studios' planned *King Kong* remake is stalled in development hell, a continuing disappointment to fans. But Pittsburgh radio-station programmer Ron Adams is gearing up to throw a Kong celebration at his second annual "Monster Bash" in June.

"He turns 65, and it's his retirement party," said Adams, who expects at least 2,000 people to honor Kong and other legendary film monsters at the second annual Monster Bash, this year being held just east of Pittsburgh, in Monroeville.

"There's a lot of strong emotional ties with Kong," Adams said. "It's almost become a religion with some people.... He was a lost soul in the world of New York City. Who really was the monster in this case?"

By Jeff Gammage. Copyright 1998, *St. Louis Post-Dispatch*.

3. SCREENPLAY: *PEACE AND QUIET*

FADE IN...
EXT. NEW YORK CITY — MORNING
Early morning light glows on the Hudson River. There is the soft sound of water lapping.
DISSOLVE TO:
Springtime trees are in blossom along the bank of the river. The scene feels like a bit of idyllic nature, quiet and serene.

The CAMERA RACKS FOCUS through the trees, to the river of cars clogging the Westside Highway. On the SOUND TRACK, the roar of city noises begins to grow.

CLOSER on the cars. The roar of the city is louder.

Vehicles and people move through the streets. The pulse of the city is louder still.

ANGLE ON canyon of buildings, the almost deafening sounds of the city ricocheting off their surfaces.

CUT TO:

INT. SUZANNE'S APARTMENT — MORNING

SUZANNE, 30s, is seated at the breakfast table, newspaper in hand, mug of tea nearby. It is a spacious apartment, big enough for two. It is also quiet, almost strangely quiet compared to the previous scene's chaos of noise.

CLOSER on Suzanne. She looks up from the paper.

SUZANNE'S POV

The river of cars down below on the Westside Highway. The outside sounds are barely a distant murmur.

BACK TO SCENE

Suzanne takes a silent sip from her mug and returns to reading the paper.

EXT. APARTMENT BUILDING — DAY

CARMEN, 20s, emerges from the rush of people on the sidewalk. Paper in hand, she is looking for an address.

CARMEN'S POV

An apartment building. The CAMERA tilts to the sky, following Carmen's gaze.

BACK TO SCENE

Carmen looks admiringly at the towering building.

HIGH ANGLE

Carmen threads her way through the crowd and enters the building. As she disappears through the doorway, the CAMERA CRANES UP and UP, as though on an elevator, and TILTS to look through an apartment window. Inside, **JULIETTE,** 30s, is dancing. Actually, she's clogging, and even through the window we can hear the rat-tat-tat of the wooden shoes over the din of the street.

INT. APARTMENT HALLWAY — DAY

Carmen comes along the hallway, closer and closer to the muffled staccato of the wooden shoes. She pauses apprehensively before the apartment door and rings the bell.

INT. JULIETTE'S APARTMENT — DAY

CLOSE ON the door as Juliette opens it to REVEAL Carmen.

CARMEN: *Hi. I'm Carmen.*

JULIETTE: *Juliette. But you know that. Come on in and I'll show you the apartment.*

REVERSE ANGLE

Carmen follows Juliette into the room. The view opens up before her.

CARMEN: *It's beautiful.*

JULIETTE: *The view? Oh yeah, it's gorgeous, but kind of pricey for one, y'know what I mean?*

Juliette flexes a leg and does a stretch as she talks.

CARMEN: *You're a dancer?*

JULIETTE: *Oh don't I wish. It's my workout. A couple of hours in the morning, a couple of hours at night if I can squeeze it in, two-three times a week. Here, sit down, why don't you. Get you anything? Coffee, tea?*

Carmen indicates a 'no' as she sits opposite Juliette. The edgy, tense strains of Vivaldi's 'Winter' from the Four Seasons CROSS FADES with their dialogue.

INSERT Carmen's POV

Juliette's knee nervously bounces up and down with the music.

CU Juliette's hands flutter with the scratchy strings.

CLOSE ON Carmen's eyes watching.

In one nonstop motion Juliette lights a cigarette and exhales with flamboyant force.

CLOSE ON Carmen watching

Juliette's feet tap-tap-tap the clogs against the hardwood floor.

INT. JULIETTE'S APARTMENT, SAME

LOW ANGLE TWO SHOT on Carmen and Juliette as the CAMERA sinks beneath the floor and travels down and diagonally through the guts of the building. Floor joists, air ducts, electrical conduits and plumbing pass by. There is a loud squawk of a parrot just before...

INT. DARRELL'S APARTMENT — DAY

THE CAMERA EMERGES from the wall to REVEAL a great African gray parrot, **ALICE**. Alice squawks again. We hold on the bird as, OFF CAMERA, there is the sound of the doorbell. Alice watches the off-camera action intently.

DARRELL: *Just a minute.*

He opens the door.

CARMEN: *Hi, I'm here about the apartment. I'm Carmen...*

DARRELL: *Oh, come in, come in.*

ANGLE ON Darrell and Carmen as they enter the room.

DARRELL: *I'm Darrell...*

The parrot squawks and whistles loudly, interrupting him.

DARRELL: *There, there, pretty girl. And this is Alice.*

CARMEN: *Alice is a bird?*

DARRELL: *Well, yeah. But she really is like a third roommate.*

Alice begins to shriek and scream in a woman's voice.

ALICE: *Help! Help me!!! No...no! Please don't, I'll do anything. PLEASE, AIIEEEE!!!*

Carmen stares, dumbfounded.

The bird clucks and ruffles its feathers.

DARRELL: *Really something, huh? She's got all these slasher movies down. But she can do barnyard animals, too. Hey, how about a chicken, Alice? Do a chicken. C'mon, girl.*

Darrell looks over to Carmen. She's gone. The door is open.

INT. APARTMENT ELEVATOR, CONTINUOUS

Carmen steps into the elevator. From down the hallway comes Alice's blood-chilling scream.

ALICE: *Not the knife. NOOOOOOO!!!!!*

DARRELL: *Alice, can't you just chill out? We're never gonna get a roommate, you keep that up.*

Carmen quickly punches a floor and the doors close.

Carmen heaves a great sigh and closes her eyes. Escape. But the elevator doors immediately open on the same floor. Darrell and Alice can still be heard from down the hallway. Alice is making chicken noises.

DARRELL: *Sure, now you do the chicken thing. Just about a minute late and eight hundred bucks a month short. Why are you so jealous?*

Carmen's eyes go wide. She double-checks the paper with the addresses written on it. Darrell slams his apartment door shut. Slowly Carmen ventures back into the hall and stops in front of the door adjacent to Darrell and Alice's.

ALICE: *Norman? Norman, is that you?*

DARRELL: *Cut it out! Just cut it out will you!*

Carmen rings the bell. The door opens to REVEAL Suzanne.

SUZANNE: *Carmen? Please, come in.*

DISSOLVE TO:

INT. SUZANNE'S APARTMENT — DAY

MONTAGE to music, with Suzanne and Carmen stand in the living room admiring the view.

Carmen and Suzanne poke their heads into Suzanne's room. It's light and airy.

Suzanne gives a quick point-by-point tour of the bathroom. Carmen checks the plumbing. Suzanne's pantomime indicates that it's redone...no leak. It's apparent that the two women have a rapport.

Carmen turns on the light in the second bedroom. She twirls in the middle of the empty room.

INT. SUZANNE'S APARTMENT — LATER

CLOSE ON tea being poured into a mug.

Suzanne and Carmen sit next to each other at the breakfast table, sharing tea. From above comes the rat-tat-tat of Juliette clogging. From next door comes the screams of Alice re-enacting another horror film.

SUZANNE: *So, I don't know about you, but I think we'd make good roommates.*

A shadow crosses Carmen's face.

CARMEN: *Actually, so do I. It's just...*

SUZANNE: *The rent?*

CARMEN: *No, it's not that. The neighbors...*

SUZANNE: *The neighbors? Oh they're fine.*

Suzanne notices Carmen's look of disbelief.

SUZANNE: *Well.... To tell the truth, I'm hard of hearing, almost deaf, really, so the neighbors can pretty much do what they like and it's not really a bother to me. Are they...?*

CARMEN: *Loud. Very.*

Above them, Juliette punctuates the conversation with an explosive cadenza of clogging.

Suzanne gives a nod and a sigh.

SUZANNE: *Do you like music?*

CARMEN: *I love music, especially classical.*

SUZANNE: *So do I.*

CARMEN: *You do? But how do you...*

SUZANNE: *Headphones. Or usually I just turn it up. Beethoven, Mahler?*

Carmen shrugs a yes, as Suzanne waves a remote in the direction of the stereo. Lush strains of Mahler come rushing through the apartment at a thunderous volume, a sonic tidal wave that overcomes every other sound.

Suzanne smiles slyly. She mouths the word "Deal?" and holds out her hand.

Carmen shakes on it.

EXT. APARTMENT BUILDING — DAY
HELICOPTER SHOT

The CAMERA pulls back from the window of Suzanne and Carmen's apartment, the two roommates still shaking hands. Juliette continues to clog away in the apartment above. Darrell berates Alice in the apartment next door. The strains of Mahler can still be heard, but are soon consumed by the ongoing roar that makes up the sounds of Manhattan. The apartment building becomes one of many in the skyline.

FADE OUT.

By Theodore Thomas. Copyright 1998, *Theodore Thomas Productions.*

1. STILL A LITTLE TOWN AFTER BIG JACKPOT

ROBY, Texas — Prosperity here began with a winning lottery ticket.

It's not the kind of prosperity that lets you build a mansion and snack on caviar. It's the kind that lets you go to sleep without tossing and turning over unpaid bills, the kind that lets you take a real vacation once a year, the kind that lets you trade a pick-up with 250,000 miles on it for one that has never been driven.

For the 43 people in this western Texas farm town who split a $46.7 million Texas lottery jackpot a year ago, that's plenty good enough.

They were, and still are, farmers and secretaries, sod busters and cotton gin feeders. Now, they're all millionaires, at least on paper.

"I sure don't feel like a millionaire," says Rex Beauchamp, who had just opened the Circle D convenience store when he added his $10 to the lottery pool last year. "I still work 60 hours a week."

But Beauchamp is out of debt, his store bought and paid for. And both his daughters' college loans are cleared off the books.

"It's changed my life, I guess," he says. "Before I worried about Social Security being there when I got old. I guess I don't worry about that too much no more."

More than anything, this first year of prosperity has taught the "Roby 43," as they have come to call themselves, just how much sweeter life can be when anything suddenly is possible.

Each member of the pool won nearly $1.1 million, paid out in 20 yearly, after-tax checks of $39,666. The payments are more than twice the annual median household income here in Fisher County, but only about $5,000 more than the annual household median income nationwide.

"It's not really enough money to call yourself rich," says Vance Lakey, a crop duster who took his wife and four daughters to Germany this Christmas. "But it is a comfort."

Virtually every one of the winners used the first check to pay off debts that had accumulated during a decade of mediocre cotton harvests. "It went right to the banker," Maxine Terry says. Her husband, Vernon "Bunny" Terry, was among 18 Terry relatives who shared in the winnings.

The only real splurge was by Shad Rasco, who works at McMurry College in Abilene. He bought a Mitsubishi 3000 Spider GT convertible for $48,000. Ever practical, the local farmers still remark on the 27-year-old's extravagance over coffee at the Silver Star cafe.

But this year of prosperity also has taught a harder lesson: No amount of money can insulate them from reality.

Last week, Peggy Dickson, the woman who organized the lottery pool, died of cancer. At age 48, she was diagnosed with an inoperable brain tumor a day before Thanksgiving, exactly one year after winning the lottery.

Dickson, a bookkeeper for her family's business, Terry's Gin, was the common denominator among lottery winners. She was the one who decided to start a pool on a lark because the jackpot had climbed to nearly $50 million. It was the only time the group bought tickets. And those who joined the pool give Dickson all the credit for their good fortune.

More than 200 people attended her funeral last Friday, two days after her second lottery check arrived in the mail. The check, like her future lottery winnings, is being handled by her estate.

"I remember her walking in here the day she bought the tickets. She was wearing a blue dress. I don't think she'd ever been in a liquor store before," says Jim Carson, the owner of Longhorn Liquors in nearby Sweetwater.

Dickson plunked down $420 in small bills and asked for 420 lottery tickets. Carson kicked in $10 of his own.

By midnight, they were rich.

"She touched the lives of 42 other people," Carson says. "She changed their lives. She changed my life, my children's lives, my children's children."

Carson went from working 80 hours a week and carrying $180,000 in debt to a work week that includes time for at least two rounds of golf, a bridge game and Friday night poker. His blood pressure dropped 60 points, although he still takes his medicine.

When he retires in five years, Carson wants to fly on the Concorde to Paris and travel to Nepal to see Mount Everest.

"I guess I'm enjoying life a lot more," he says.

Carson not only won a share of the jackpot, he also won a $460,000 commission from the state for selling the winning ticket. And his lottery sales have exploded since then. He is now the 113th top seller among 17,500 Texas lottery retailers, up from 5,534th.

For many here, the winning lottery ticket was just the first sign of a new run of desperately needed good luck.

Roby once was a thriving town of 1,200 people with a shopping district, three cafes, a movie theater and a motel. Today, the town population has fallen to 616 people. Almost every storefront is boarded over. The theater is long gone, the motel grown over with weeds.

But this year brought a bumper cotton crop, after 15 poor years bedeviled by boll weevil infestations.

Beneath soft blue skies, the red fields are picked clean of cotton. The two gins in Fisher County are working overtime to process more than 50,000 bales of cotton — twice the yield of last year's crop — before year's end.

The dollars from the harvest will roll over three or four times, to the gins, seed and fertilizer suppliers, stores, banks, even the restaurants.

"In a town like Roby," says Kevin Brinkley, an economist with the National Cotton Council of America, "that's huge."

While the cotton crop may have a greater effect on Roby than the lottery, it's clear that the first winnings sparked an urban renewal of sorts.

Homes are spruced up inside and out. Thurman Terry replaced his carpet. Several houses are wearing new coats of paint. Don Campbell is considering building a new house.

New trucks are everywhere.

Replacing hard-working pickups was the most common splurge among lottery winners. Brad Stuart, a rancher, traded in his battered old Chevy with 250,000 miles on the odometer. The most difficult decision was choosing the color of a new truck. He settled on red.

The lottery money also has allowed two new businesses to keep the doors open: Beauchamp's store and Manny Valdez's restaurant, Susie's Fish and Grill, named for his wife.

And most of the farmers and ranchers have paid off bank notes, allowing themselves to plant a few more acres a little thicker with seed and fertilizer. Buddy Williamson bought another quarter-section of grazing land to increase his herd of cattle.

But Roby still looks like a town that has seen its heyday come and go.

Those who stay here do so because they like being able to leave the car keys in the ignition and the doors to the house unlocked. They like going to the grocery store and knowing nearly every other shopper.

A winning lottery ticket didn't change that.

"We're still the same little town we always were," says "Little Mike" Terry. "We just worry a little less."

By Debbie Howlett. Copyright 1997, *USA Today*.

1. MOZART

Some psychologists do not agree that a few people have an innate talent that allows them to excel at an early age. For example, they believe that the musical genius of Mozart was largely due to his father and about 10,000 hours of piano practice. Professor Michael Howe claims that hard work and domineering parents create child prodigies. Furthermore, he says that the belief in an innate gift is hurting thousands of children who are not given opportunities in the arts and sports.

Almost three-quarters of music teachers believe a child is incapable of doing well unless he or she shows a specific musical talent from an early age. "But for every child identified as having an innate talent and who is given encouragement and facilities, there are those who are not and who are thus being sold short, denied, excluded, shut out," Professor Howe told the British Psychological Society conference in Brighton, England. He went on: "That is a powerful reason for saying we need to look into the validity of these assumptions. Unless you can show that innate talent exists, then it is probably better to assume it doesn't."

Hard evidence of great talent in childhood is difficult to come by, he added. "A young child who has never seen a piano, walks up to it and starts to do wonderful things, that is something we would accept as innate. There are a lot of stories about people like this. However, when they are investigated, they are almost always found to be untrue."

Professor Howe, his colleague at Exeter University, U.K., Dr. Jane Davidson, and Professor John Sloboda from Keele University, U.K., at first studied only young musicians but have now included talented children in other fields. Parental support from an early age and around 10,000 hours of practice were fundamental requirements for a child prodigy, he said.

"Mozart could not have been Mozart without practice. His early years were unusual for a child, and his father [Leopold, who was also a musician] was similar to parents of successful young musicians now. Parental support is tremendously important."

"Idiot savants" — mentally retarded children or young adults who are usually autistic, but who show a particular ability or skill — come closest to the idea of innate talent, Professor Howe said. Stephen Wiltshire, the young artist whose intricate architectural drawings have amazed the art world, is an example of this.

Professor Howe said that all children are born different and there are many reasons why they do not have the same chance of succeeding. However, he believes that the idea of innate talent is negative, and hurts thousands of children who are being labeled incapable for no reason.

By Liz Hunt. Copyright 1996.

2. Learning Style Questionnaire

This questionnaire has been designed to help you identify the way(s) you learn best — the way(s) you *prefer* to learn.

DIRECTIONS:

Read each statement on the following pages. Please respond to the statements AS THEY APPLY TO YOUR STUDY OF ENGLISH.

Decide whether you agree or disagree with each statement. For example, if you *strongly agree,* circle *"SA."*

Please respond to each statement quickly, without too much thought. Try not to change your answers after you choose them. Please answer all the questions.

> Key: SA = strongly agree   A = agree
>   U = undecided   D = disagree
>   SD = strongly disagree

1. When the teacher tells me the instructions, I understand better.   SA A U D SD

2. I prefer to learn by doing something in class.   SA A U D SD

3. I get more work done when I work with others.   SA A U D SD

4. I learn more when I study with a group.   SA A U D SD

5. In class, I learn best when I work with others.   SA A U D SD

6. I learn better by reading what the teacher writes on the board.   SA A U D SD

7. When someone tells me how to do something, I learn it better.   SA A U D SD

8. When I do things in class, I learn better.   SA A U D SD

9. I remember things I've heard better than things I've read.   SA A U D SD

10. When I read instructions, I remember them better.   SA A U D SD

11. I learn more when I can make a model of something.   SA A U D SD

12. I understand better when I read instructions.   SA A U D SD

Now turn the page.

13. When I study alone, I remember things better. SA A U D SD

14. I learn more when I make something for a class project. SA A U D SD

15. I enjoy learning in class by doing experiments. SA A U D SD

16. I learn better when I make drawings as I study. SA A U D SD

17. I learn better in class when the teacher gives a lecture. SA A U D SD

18. When I work alone, I learn better. SA A U D SD

19. I understand things better in class when I participate in a role-play. SA A U D SD

20. I learn better in class when I listen to someone. SA A U D SD

21. I enjoy working on an assignment with two or three classmates. SA A U D SD

22. When I build something, I remember what I have learned better. SA A U D SD

23. I prefer to study with others. SA A U D SD

24. I learn better by reading than by listening to someone. SA A U D SD

25. I enjoy making something for a class project. SA A U D SD

26. I learn best in class when I can participate in related activities. SA A U D SD

27. In class, I work better when I work alone. SA A U D SD

28. I prefer working on projects by myself. SA A U D SD

29. I learn more by reading textbooks than by listening to lectures. SA A U D SD

30. I prefer to work by myself. SA A U D SD

SELF-SCORING SHEET

Instructions

There are 5 questions for each learning category in this questionnaire. The questions are grouped below according to each learning style. Each question you answer has a numerical value.

SA = 5   A = 4   U = 3   D = 2   SD = 1

Fill in the blanks below with the numerical value of each answer. For example, if you answered Strongly Agree (SA) for question 6 (a visual question), write a number 5 (SA) on the blank next to question 6 below.

Visual

6 - _5_

When you have completed all the numerical values for *Visual*, add the numbers. Multiply the answer by 2, and put the total in the appropriate blank.

Follow this process for each of the learning style categories. When you are finished, look at the scale at the bottom of the page; it will help you determine your major learning style preference(s), your minor learning style preference(s), and those learning style(s) that are negligible (you can ignore them).

If you need help, please ask your teacher.

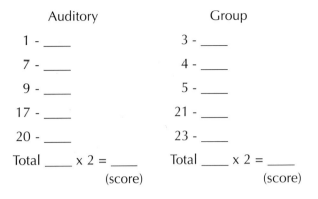

Auditory	Group
1 - ____	3 - ____
7 - ____	4 - ____
9 - ____	5 - ____
17 - ____	21 - ____
20 - ____	23 - ____
Total ____ x 2 = ____ (score)	Total ____ x 2 = ____ (score)

Kinesthetic	Individual
2 - ____	13 - ____
8 - ____	18 - ____
15 - ____	27 - ____
19 - ____	28 - ____
26 - ____	20 - ____
Total ____ x 2 = ____ (score)	Total ____ x 2 = ____ (score)

Major Learning Style Preference	38 - 50
Minor Learning Style Preference	25 - 37
Negligible	0 - 24

By Joy Reid. Copyright 1984.

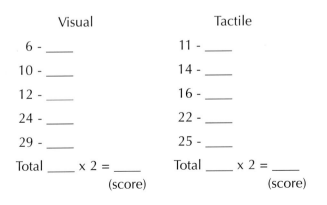

Visual	Tactile
6 - ____	11 - ____
10 - ____	14 - ____
12 - ____	16 - ____
24 - ____	22 - ____
29 - ____	25 - ____
Total ____ x 2 = ____ (score)	Total ____ x 2 = ____ (score)

CREDITS